CHILD DEATH
INVESTIGATIONS

CHILD DEATH INVESTIGATIONS

Interdisciplinary Techniques from Cradle to Court

SECOND EDITION

Lisa Mayhew

CAROLINA ACADEMIC PRESS

Durham, North Carolina

Library of Congress Cataloging-in-Publication Data

Mayhew, Lisa.
 Child death investigations : interdisciplinary techniques from cra-
dle to court / Lisa Mayhew. -- 2nd ed.
     p. cm.
 Includes bibliographical references and index.
 ISBN 978-1-61163-176-0 (alk. paper)
 1. Child abuse--Investigation. 2. Children--Death. 3. Children's
accidents. 4. Sudden death in children. 5. Infanticide. 6. Chil-
dren--Suicidal behavior. 7. Homicide investigation. I. Title.

 HV8079.C46M39 2012
 363.25'952--dc23   2012021317

Carolina Academic Press
700 Kent Street
Durham, North Carolina 27701
Telephone (919) 489-7486
Fax (919) 493-5668
www.cap-press.com

Printed in the United States of America

CONTENTS

Acknowledgments

I am fortunate to work for a wonderful group of forensic pathologists who always take the time to share their knowledge and experience with me. My thanks also go out to the many and varied professionals for all that they do with regards to children. A special thank you goes to Don Rabon for his continuous encouragement and support, Krista Ragan for being such a valuable colleague and editor, and friends and family for their support and understanding on the bad days.

CHILD DEATH INVESTIGATIONS

CHAPTER 1

INTRODUCTION

One of the virtues of being very young is that you don't let the facts get in the way of your imagination.

— Sam Levenson

"How do you do your job?" It is a question I hear often. It is a question I, in turn, ask sex abuse detectives, defense attorneys, and entomologists. We all have our passion in life, and I have found mine in the investigation of child deaths. While I never expect others to share my passion or intensity for child death investigations, it is important for them to gain a greater understanding of these cases and a deeper respect for what they require.

This book is an attempt to do just that, to educate and explain the process of investigating child deaths. Each chapter will explore specific causes and manners of death, while at the same time detailing investigative questions, strategies, and, scene considerations. The death of a child initiates an investigative response from a number of agencies. Beginning with the 911 call, through the autopsy, and then into the courtroom, professionals from various disciplines seek answers for their own purposes. We will address those disciplines and explore their investigative roles and responsibilities across the five manners of death.

The professional community tends to emphasize only certain types of deaths, such as Sudden Infant Death Syndrome (SIDS) and homicides of children. This tendency is reflected in existing checklists that focus on injuries and infants, law enforcement death investigation procedures limited to adult deaths or child abuse, and a general lack of information about the other types of child deaths that occur more often. A comprehensive work on child death investigation has not previously been available. Regardless of the level of experience or particular discipline, this book will prepare professionals for any type of child death investigation, from the onset to the outcome.

Before we get started, readers must shed preconceived notions. The goals of this book are not just to educate professionals about child deaths and to improve investigations but also to change perceptions and mindsets. A critical difference between adult deaths and child deaths is how we perceive them. We tend to think of adult deaths in terms of what and whom, and child deaths in terms of why and how. Remember this important rule:

> Investigations are not conducted based on what the manner is *assumed* to be; rather the most appropriate determinations of cause and manner of death are based on a thorough, interdisciplinary investigation.

For the purposes of this book, *child* is defined as individuals from birth through seventeen years of age. There will be an emphasis on infants less than one year of age since that is where a large number of fatalities, as well as mistakes and controversy, occur. Numbers of child fatalities tend to decrease during the school-age years and then increase again in the fourteen to seventeen years age range. The types of deaths observed also vary across ages. The following chapters are organized by manner of death so that the various means of death and the ages at which they occur can be properly addressed. While it may seem to contradict the above rule, organizing the book by manner of death demonstrates the importance of the investigation in reaching the final determinations of cause and manner of death. Reaching the appropriate determination of cause and manner is particularly important given the similar causes, circumstances, and histories child death cases can present. The case examples and exercises are not only designed to enable readers to process the different avenues one case history can take but also demonstrate how proper inquiries can eliminate and confirm possibilities.

It is not possible to cover every way child fatalities occur. Consequently, this book serves as a comprehensive view of appropriate investigative approaches that can be used for most any child death case. However, investigators should always be prepared to "step out of the box" and modify inquiries to suit the needs of a particular case.

CHAPTER 2

CONSIDERATIONS AND CHALLENGES

Any fact facing us is not as important as our attitude toward it, for that determines our success or failure. The way you think about a fact may defeat you before you ever do anything about it. You are overcome by the fact because you think you are.

— Norman Vincent Peale

Every child death case gets full attention at the onset, period. There are no exceptions. Once an investigation has been initiated and the baseline information gathered, the investigator can pursue whichever direction the information indicates. For law enforcement, investigating child deaths requires a change in the mindset of "treat everything like a homicide until proven otherwise." The reason for such a change is two-fold. First, statistically, the majority of cases are likely accidental or natural. Second, when solid foundations for every case are established, mistakes are minimized and homicides are less likely to be missed. When the assumption of homicide is made in a case, before all the facts are established, the critical details necessary for determining the cause and manner of death are not gathered.

Investigative Base

A critical part of every case is its history. Remember rule #2 when dealing with children:

> Regardless of age, they do not live in a vacuum. They exist in a system, and that entire system must be taken into account during the course of an investigation.

The immediate and extended history can provide the pertinent information needed for the determination of cause and manner. Because so many child deaths are sudden and unexpected, there may be little or no history that caregivers are able to provide.

A solid investigative base will include the following:

- Demographics—The caregivers and their relationships to the child, all siblings.
- Investigating agency—The lead agency and investigator and contact information; how notification of the death was made; first responders and contact information.
- Scenes—The location of the death, the positions of the decedent, the activities surrounding the death, observations of the scene.
- Past medical history—Including the contact information for the treating physicians or related providers.
- Immediate history and circumstances of the death—The investigator's compass, pointing in the direction the investigation needs to follow.

Regardless of the child's age or the circumstances of the death, this information provides a base from which investigators can launch. Based on answers and findings at this point, more specific and directed inquires may be made. Weak foundations can lead to cracks, instability, and collapse of structures, and the same holds true for investigations.

Challenges

While many child death cases share similarities, they can each present unique challenges. Never make the mistake of saying "I've seen it all," because you may encounter the case that defies all logic. With that in mind, we will discuss some of the typical challenges observed in the investigation of child deaths.

Lies can come in many forms, from little white ones to blatant deceptions. Families can be the most prolific liars, but not always in a negative way. Put yourself in their shoes for one minute. Someone comes to your door, into your home, and asks personal and possibly invasive questions about your family. What would be your first response? Initially, most of you would be guarded and say little. That is an honest and natural response. The demeanor and approach by the investigator will have considerable influence at this stage. From working these cases over the years, experienced investigators have learned the importance of sensitivity and patience with families. Another lie told by caregivers, commonly heard in accidental child deaths is, "I was only on the phone for a minute," when the evidence suggests a significantly longer timeframe. While the apparent inconsistency can shed a negative light initially, it is an honest response, since it only felt like a minute to the caregiver at the time. But what feels like an eternity is the time it takes to locate the child. Those who have experienced a child getting away from them understand this concept. The bottom line is the lie is not an intentional deception, and if patiently guided, the caregivers will generally expand the timeframe to appropriately fit the circumstances. The "true" lies will typically be apparent from the onset through inconsistent histories, physical evidence, or autopsy findings.

Along the same lines as little lies, we examine the art of minimizing. Typically initiated by the statement, "I was just," minimizing provides a glimpse into the truth behind the circumstances. Examples of minimizing include:

- I only/just shook him/her to wake him/her up;
- I only/just hit him/her to get him/her to breathe;

- I only/just squeezed a little;
- I was just playing/bouncing/tossing him/her when he/she *might* have hit her head.

At face value, these explanations are admissions of guilt. They may be admitting that something definitely occurred, that he or she was responsible, and how the event may have happened. The "how" is often suggested by trigger words such as *hit, smack,* and *shake.* When handled properly, these initial admissions can ultimately lead to full confessions. However, there is a flip side to this coin. The caregiver providing the history may be exaggerating what they actually did. What does that mean? It means that a parent or caregiver who does not use their hands as a form of discipline or correction with their child views hitting or smacking as a bad or hurtful thing to do to a child. So when they demonstrate 'hit,' 'smack,' or 'shake,' it resembles more of a 'tap,' or 'wiggle.' Nonetheless, *to them* it felt worse and they may believe they actually hurt the child. Think about it this way, if someone says 'there was blood all over the bathroom' our expectation is 'spatter' when the reality is a 'droplet.'

A common minimization occurs concerning the use of CPR and other resuscitative measures. It is possible that CPR did occur or was attempted, and the efforts were done with the best of intentions under the circumstances. A contradicting scenario involves the "CPR crutch," which a suspect will lean heavily on until he or she falls over. This "crutch," when used deceptively, is often found in conjunction with the statement, "I was just," and is typically used as an excuse to explain visible trauma or bruises. A good way to determine fact from fiction is to obtain a reconstruction of attempts from caregivers. Honest attempts at CPR will be reconstructed in a straightforward manner, while deceptive individuals will have to create, and not reconstruct the incident since it did not actually occur. Often the deceptive reconstructions will demonstrate a hint of what actually happened to the child. There is no substitute for a solid reconstruction in an investigation.

Unfortunately, eyewitnesses to the actual death of children are uncommon. Many deaths are not witnessed as the child is found unresponsive or already deceased, and the scene of the death and history behind it typically provide the circumstances. This is often the case with natural, accidental, and suicidal deaths. Homicides are different since typically the only person to witness the death is the perpetrator. Sadly, most children are killed in their own homes, by a parent or relative, with no one else within sight or within the scene. Consequently, there may not be another person to provide incriminating information against the perpetrator. An additional complication arises when caretakers cover for each other, sometimes making it quite difficult to determine who actually inflicted the fatal injuries. The investigator must make sure he or she has the most, as well as the most accurate, information going into any interview with or interrogation of a suspect. It is critical that the investigator establish who was with the child when the symptoms began or were first observed, or when the child became unresponsive. Prosecutors can use that information to establish custody and control of the child at the time, which may prove enough for charges. Pathologists can determine if the information provided is consistent or inconsistent with the autopsy findings.

Prosecutors know the challenges they face in child death cases. But these challenges can affect an investigation from a variety of perspectives, whether or not charges are applicable. There are several additional challenges that can cause problems for multiple agencies. The subtlety of the child's injuries can sometimes result in a diagnosis of undetermined cause of death which can hamper the ability of agencies to pursue further action on a case. For example, child protection services could be seeking to remove existing children from the home but a ruling of undetermined may not give them the evidence they need to do so. The inexperience of some doctors can lead to mistakes, typically in the form of failing to notify the proper authorities either of the child's death or of suspicious injuries. Those types of mistakes can often be costly, since they compromise the investigation at the onset.

Notification delays are problematic enough; however, delays in seeking treatment and delays in the onset of symptoms or death are critical investigative hurdles. Caretakers may discount injuries not immediately visible and may not seek treatment until symptoms become obvious. Other caretakers may do so deliberately. Regardless, the end result can be difficulty in determining the timing of the injury. Delays can also mean adding settings (i.e., scenes) and individuals to a timeline.

Cases involving more than one scene can sometimes be attributed to the portability factor. For example, there are many products designed for toting around the smallest of children. Whether in a stroller, infant carrier, or sling, if the child is adequately covered, it becomes difficult to observe the child's condition. Unresponsive or deceased children can look like sleeping children when observed at a glance. The timeline surrounding the death needs to specifically address locations and if the child was seen to be active or responsive at any time in each setting.

Scenes

The first action an investigator should perform is to make sure that the scene (or scenes) is properly secured. A scene typically gets compromised in one of two ways: either there is no (or a delayed) notification or first responding officers follow the ambulance to the hospital. The investigator should examine agency protocols and guidelines to ensure specific procedures address this issue. Standard procedure should dictate that first responding officers remain at the scene, dispatching investigators to the hospital when applicable. Interviews should be conducted with everyone who was at the location at the time and who responded to the location. In addition, interviews should be conducted with all medical personnel who worked on the child at the original scene and at the hospital (when appropriate). In the majority of cases, there will be two scenes to cover, the original scene of death and the hospital. Occasionally caregivers will transport the child privately to the hospital. Photographs from each scene will be beneficial to the pathologists and should be shared with them as quickly as feasible. Measurements from the scene can be compared to the child's body measurements taken at the autopsy to confirm or refute a history.

High target areas within scenes for processing are feeding areas, bathrooms, and anywhere clothing may be kept. Kitchens and bathrooms are prime areas for the proverbial last good nerve to be stepped on, and there are many environmental weapons within an arm's reach. Regardless of the circumstances surrounding a child's death, a common denominator across histories is vomiting. Investigators should check clothing, bedding, hampers, and washers for clothing items that may contain vomit, if not visible in the scene. Histories could also include toileting accidents. This is evidence that could also confirm or refute a history. Do not forget the reconstruction!

Ideally, the scenes are processed within twenty-four hours after the initial response, barring any notification problems. Most professionals reading this book have gone into private residences as part of the job. It is important for them to avoid judgments and assumptions based on initial reactions. From an investigative perspective, it is important to consider the impression of the total scene given the knowledge that a child lived in that environment. Does the investigator get the impression that the scene is a child friendly environment? Housekeeping may not necessarily be a priority, but the child is well cared for. The investigator should learn to think and absorb surroundings from a child's point of view.

Body Exams

The less done to a body at the scene, and prior to the autopsy, the better. It is important to document carefully whatever is done to the body and to provide that information to the pathologist conducting the autopsy. He or she will need to match any findings on the body with anything done to the body during handling or processing. This documentation should be obtained from the person who first found the body, and be done by all first responders to the scene, all personnel who process and investigate the scene, and the transporters. Typical guidelines include the following:

- Know the jurisdictional statutes pertaining to the body.
- Know pronouncement statutes so that unnecessary handling and resuscitative measures are avoided.

- Law enforcement should know what procedures can be performed at the autopsy, such as gunshot residue and fingerprinting, and whether the pathologist prefers to have such procedures done at the time of the autopsy or at the scene.
- Ensure that anything touching the body goes with the body.
- Make sure all photographs are taken of the original position of the body.
- Hospital personnel should take measures to ensure no unnecessary handling of a body after death is pronounced.
- Document all items removed from the body at the scene in order to preserve the evidence prior to transport.
- Do not leave a body at the scene for an extended period of time.
- Once the body is photographed and appropriately processed, it should be removed and taken to the morgue.

Weapons

The weapon or weapons involved in the death of a child can be found in his or her own environment. The weapon could be the actual environment itself, such as water in a drowning death of a child. In a case where the weapon is unknown, it is critical to examine the scene carefully for possibilities. In a case involving toxins, toxicological analyses can be performed, but it is beneficial to provide investigative details to allow the toxicologists to perform the appropriate tests. Unfortunately, when stationary weapons such as walls, doors, tables, and porcelain are used against a child, there may not be any visible evidence.

The Autopsy

There are two types of autopsies performed in child death investigations. The forensic autopsy may be the most important piece of evidence in an investigation. The extent of the autopsy will be dictated by the circumstances, with some cases receiving only external exams and toxicology, and others receiving a full postmortem examination. For example, all infants may receive a full forensic autopsy, while a victim of a motor vehicle crash may get only an external exam and have samples drawn for toxicology. Additional procedures may be done on a case-by-case basis, and protocols will differ across pathological practices and medical examiner and coroner offices. For law enforcement, nothing can replace the opportunity to exchange information with pathologists at the time of the autopsy. When that is not possible, ongoing communication can keep investigations running smoothly and can potentially expedite the final determinations of cause and manner of death. Other professionals should never be afraid to ask questions regarding the autopsy results. I encourage those professionals that deal directly with the families to discuss the results with the doctors so that the interpretation of results to the family is accurate.

The second type of autopsy performed involves dissecting the social environment of the child. It is, in a sense, a systemic autopsy: we always examine the system the child exists in during the course of an investigation. This systemic autopsy of the child's social environment includes the following:

- Who lives with the child on a full-time basis? This includes all those living in the primary residence.
- Who is at the residence on a regular basis? This includes all those that stay overnight regularly or are at the residence more than three or four days a week.
- Define the relationships of those caregivers living in the residence. This can get confusing! Determine if caretakers are married, living together, boyfriend/girlfriend, friend, or other.
- Who is present that should/should not be? This is a communication issue. Suppose child protection services (CPS) has a protection plan in place that prohibits Crazy Uncle Frank from being with the children unsupervised. A patrol officer responds to a car break-in at the residence. That patrol officer knows nothing about the protection plan, and thus has no reason to notify CPS that Crazy Uncle Frank is there with the children. Now flip the coin: the CPS worker responds to a report about

children being left alone at the residence. They arrive to find the children being supervised by an adult (Crazy Uncle Frank). Unfortunately, they have no knowledge of the restraining order against Crazy Uncle Frank. *Communication!*

- Who is *not* there? Who was left to supervise the children but is nowhere to be found? Or who was heard on the 911 call but is not at the scene when first responders arrived?
- Determine all known children. Be sure to find out all known children of the caregivers. Children by different mothers or fathers could have different names in different counties or states. There could be a relevant history concerning those children that could prove valuable to the death investigation.
- Determine if there are any histories with other agencies. A history check should be done with the appropriate agencies, which could include child protection services, domestic violence agencies, mental health agencies, schools, and home visitors.

Summary

Checklists and guidelines that are specifically designed for child death investigations exist across the country. As good as they may be, they cannot capture all of the details for every case. While this text is comprehensive, it will only prepare professionals for what they will typically encounter. There is no easy way to cover *all* possible circumstances and scenarios that investigators will deal with in child fatalities. The easiest way to summarize the best approach to child death investigations is the totality of evidence. The scenes, statements, histories, pathology, toxicology, and agencies must all be part of the equation. Every case will be different but still requires all of these areas to be addressed to varying degrees. Any cases that start as unknowns or unexpected and any suspicious cases should cover all areas comprehensively. Cases where the circumstances are apparent at the onset, such as some accidents or suicides, may focus more heavily on other areas. Professionals have to think on their feet and learn to be flexible with their approaches.

I have included an investigative "to do" list at the end of chapters four through eight that can be incorporated into a death scene/investigation checklist. Agencies can develop these checklists to suit their own needs and cases. Based on my experience, the best advice is to keep a checklist short and easy to complete. No one wants to write paragraphs in the middle of a scene. Check boxes, multiple choices, and areas for notes seem to appeal to professionals the most. Given the high emotions that accompany these cases, an investigator should consider what will be easiest to gather from the family under the circumstances. If a family feels uncomfortable with the questions, particularly when being questioned by law enforcement, it may help ease their concerns if they understand that the information will help the pathologist determine exactly what happened to their child.

CHAPTER 3

INTERDISCIPLINARY COLLABORATION

Minds are like parachutes—they only function when open.
—Thomas Dewar

When emphasizing the importance of interdisciplinary approaches to child death investigations, I go back to my roots as a child development specialist. Consider a child with special needs and the number of professionals involved in the care, education, and treatment of that child's specific needs. The list will likely include parents, teachers, occupational therapists, physical therapists, speech therapists, early interventionists, nurses, and medical specialists. If one member of this team is not communicating regularly and collaborating with the other members, the risk to the child could be significant. Not only would gaps in services occur but also duplications, with potentially harmful results.

Now, consider a child that has passed away. With the family at the core of any investigation, the professionals and agencies involved could include most or all of the following:

- Emergency medical services
- Hospital personnel
- Physicians and/or pediatricians
- Law enforcement
- Child protection services
- Mental health
- Schools
- Medical examiners/Pathologists/Coroners
- Medicolegal death investigators

- Prosecutors
- Defense attorneys

It takes only one agency or professional that does not communicate effectively during the investigation of a child death to negatively impact the course of the investigation, the outcome of the investigation, or possibly both. Anything less than full collaboration across professions is unacceptable. Collectively, we are their last voice so check your egos and politics at the door.

Interdisciplinary versus Multidisciplinary

The term *multidisciplinary* is applied to the child fatality review teams established across the country. Their primary role is to review the deaths of children and identify trends in fatalities, to recommend policy and/or legislative changes aimed at preventing future fatalities, and to identify and address systemic issues in cases. Thus, the term is appropriate since "many" disciplines bring their information to the table for discussion and analysis.

Multiple, or many, disciplines providing information is one matter; however, many disciplines investigating as well as gathering and sharing information at the same time is an entirely different matter. Multidisciplinary approaches result in parallel investigations where information and efforts are not shared and can conflict with one another; as a result, there is no active communication. All information gathered should be appropriately shared, and all investigative efforts must be coordinated. Multidisciplinary investigations simply do not work. Child death investigations *must* be interdisciplinary.

Interdisciplinary approaches for child death investigations are necessary for several reasons. Most important, no agency can successfully complete an investigation by its efforts alone. It is not possible. Second, communication with a family is critical during the course of an investigation. For example, how, what, and when information is shared with and conveyed to the family in the investigation of a suspicious death can be critical to the outcome of the case. The contacts with the family, at this point potential suspects, have to be coordinated. The same principle applies when investigating a non-suspicious death. Reaching the determinations of cause and manner of death depends heavily on the proper gathering of specific details. A significant number of those details may come from the family. It is unnecessary for several different agencies vying for similar information each to make contact with and interview families. Such an approach creates undue stress on a family experiencing a terrible loss. Every attempt should be made to coordinate the gathering and sharing of information that minimizes stress on the family while maximizing the amount of information obtained.

Mandates

Many of the agencies involved in the investigation of a child death will have mandates that dictate their duties, abilities, and authority. Mandates will also specify how and what types of information are shared for certain agencies. It is important for professionals to understand specifically what other professionals are responsible for during the course of an investigation. Coordinating and conducting an investigation into the death of a child is a stressful event for any professional. Knowing what other agencies will be doing, and why, will ensure a cohesive investigation, avoid conflicts during the investigation, and create a solid interdisciplinary foundation for future investigations.

Respect for Professional Boundaries

A common problem occurs in death investigations involving children when professionals step on each other's toes. Too many hands in the cookie jar, so to speak. Tension runs at full throttle, and everyone is trying to get answers or place blame. But each professional involved must stay within the bounds of his or her role and authority.

These types of mistakes will directly and indirectly affect the course and outcome of an investigation. For example, a social worker tells a person indirectly involved in a case that he is a suspect and should get a lawyer. Flag on the play! As a result, the individual, who was scheduled for a polygraph to eliminate him from the timeline and who was not a suspect, retains a lawyer and refuses the polygraph. Indirect effects are manifested through the deterioration of working relationships, which lead to lack of communication and collaboration on future cases. Some of this may be due to personality conflicts. However, if a classroom of two-year-old children can figure out how to get along in the sandbox, I feel sure adults can as well.

Identify and Define

Since all jurisdictions function differently, agency roles for child death investigations must be defined based on identified needs. Needs are typically identified in one of two ways. First, when a problem occurs during an investigation. Problems such as these must be dealt with at the time to prevent future occurrences. Second, issues are identified through the child death review process. Depending on when the review occurs in relation to the death, solutions and recommendations may be retrospective.

Common areas of need include communication and notification. Enhancing communication across agencies has a tendency to lessen or eliminate other problem areas during an investigation. Notification issues can create a snowball effect that can effectively bury a case if not dealt with immediately. For every need or issue identified, a solution must be provided and implemented. Otherwise, the same problem will potentially reoccur in future death investigations.

Defined roles may take the form of guidelines, policy changes, protocols, or legislative changes. However the case may be, every agency affected by the change should agree to the implementation of the change. In essence, multidisciplinary recommendations should have multidisciplinary approval that results in interdisciplinary application. If there is no "trickle down" effect of recommendations to the front line agency personnel, collaborative efforts are futile.

Resources

An advantage to working child death cases is that the resources available to professionals are extensive. Regardless of the type of death, investigators will find information and assistance from a variety of sources. Potential sources could include the following:

- Other local and state agencies—governmental or private
- Medical specialists
- Therapists
- Advocacy groups or centers
- Foundations and professional associations
- Support groups
- Private consultants

The first priority would be to identify resources in your own backyard that are easily accessible and available to investigators. Not only may they provide helpful general information, but depending on the type of resource, they may have specific information regarding that particular child or family (e.g., day care licensing agencies, physicians, or mental health professionals). Investigators should never feel that they are on their own during an investigation. Familiarize yourself with what is available with regards to the individual case and arm yourself with every piece of knowledge available.

Stress Management

This is one area that every professional involved in the investigation of child fatalities needs to absorb into his or her daily life. Whether through personal approaches or professional assistance, something should be employed to debrief oneself after an investigation. If your agency does not have some type of critical stress management program, find an outside source. While time management is a staple of stress management techniques, we can never predict when a death will occur or how long an investigation will take. Any type of case can test even the most seasoned investigator. Find an appropriate outlet for your stress, or it can compromise your objectivity and focus.

Summary

One of the keys to understanding interdisciplinary collaboration is appreciating that other professionals are viewing the same case through different lenses. Not the wrong lens or a cloudy lens, but a different lens. While the perspectives may differ, we are all essentially working toward the same goal, which is the protection and advocacy for children. Taking the steps to know what agency mandates are, collaborating on roles, and sharing information will go a long way toward the successful conclusion of a child death investigation. Another important aspect for agencies to respect is training. If it is determined that an agency is in need of training in a certain area, there is only one solution. *Get the agency trained!* The worst thing any agency or professional can do is criticize another and do nothing to fix the problem. Put up or shut up as they say. Stress on the job is what we signed on for. The jobs we do, by definition, imply stress. However, if you ever reach the level of burnout, turn that pager in. You run the risk of becoming part of the problem instead of the solution. The bottom line is simple: the playground is big enough for everyone so do not throw sand at your friends.

CHAPTER 4

NATURAL

And it is still true, no matter how old you are—when you go out into the world, it is best to hold hands and stick together.

—Robert Fulghum

Four-month-old male was last seen alive at approximately 10:30 a.m. when fed. Put down for nap and found unresponsive at 12:20. No past medical history. No signs of foul play.

The above history is a typical account of many natural deaths presenting for autopsy. Thousands of children and infants die unexpectedly each year from various natural causes. Infants who are amazingly resilient yet vulnerable, older children who are vibrant and blooming, and athletic adolescents, all can fall victim to the undetected. Common causes can include pneumonia/bronchopneumonia, sepsis/infection, myocarditis, complications of prematurity, congenital anomalies, seizure disorders, other respiratory and cardiac diseases, and Sudden Infant Death Syndrome. The bottom line is the illness or condition may not have presented as serious, or was not known to exist prior to the death.

Now the investigation begins. Typically, the histories associated with these deaths are benign; there is little information to gather because nothing happened prior to finding the child unresponsive. The three key investigative areas to consider with natural deaths are the circumstances, the medical history, and the environment.

Circumstances

The initial history associated with a case is often the first glimpse of the circumstances surrounding the death. It is generally a 'negative' history since the caregivers discover the child unresponsive or witness them collapse. Varying scenarios can present, such as children playing or engaging in everyday activities or athletics and collapsing. Sudden deaths from acute onset of illness or lengthy illness occur less often but provide concrete medical circumstances.

From a medicolegal perspective, the circumstances surrounding the death and prior to the death are crucial. Medical examiners, coroners and pathologists will want to know:

- What was the child/infant doing when it was last seen alive? (eating, playing, skating, running, crying, etc.)*
- What had the child/infant been doing in the previous 24–48 hours?
  - Typical routines/settings
  - Typical feeding
  - Any variations in routines, recent trips, or new caregivers?
- Any physical complaints from the child or symptoms of illness?

* Note that the time the child/infant was last seen alive does NOT include when they were last checked and 'looked' like or 'appeared' to be sleeping. Deceased or unresponsive children/infants can look like they are sleeping. It is important to document the time last seen alive as when the child was engaged in an activity, such as eating or playing.

The above considerations will have a different significance for different ages and should be addressed accordingly. Answers to these questions will provide indicators of possible findings at autopsy, as well as guide further examination into other investigative areas.

Medical History

When the circumstances appear negative, the next logical place to seek information is the child's medical history. Investigators should begin with the most recent history and work backwards. In the event the child is transported to the hospital, the emergency room records will be the immediate pertinent medical history. Combining that information with the circumstances may provide the necessary answers to coincide with the autopsy, regardless of age; however, if it does not then continue probing. Next, the investigator needs to determine the child's primary pediatrician/ physician, the date the child was last seen and request records for that date. Any concerns or issues from that visit and up to the date of death should be documented. If no concerns or issues exist, request records from the date last seen and prior, documenting any history of illness, injury or diagnoses. In cases involving infants, these records will also provide a history of well-child checks and immunizations. If a history of hospitalization is found, determine when and where the child was hospitalized and request records.

After examining the first part of the medical history, it may be necessary to look at the birth history in applicable cases. Given that *all* births are traumatic, examine the history for any extenuating circumstances prior to, during and after the birth that could have affected the infant. Complications such as breech position, cord complications or complications with the mother that may have necessitated an early delivery should be documented.

Now the investigator should have a complete picture of the decedent medically, from day one up to the time of death. There is still more to gather prior to the birth in the form of a prenatal history. Ideally, that history is available if the mother sought prenatal care. Unfortunately, not all women get prenatal care, while others may not be aware they *are* pregnant until shortly before the birth. If the prenatal history is present it becomes an additional piece of the investigation. Examine the prenatal course for any complications that may have occurred, with the mother and the baby's health.

The medical history of the family can also be valuable. It will be important to document any known existing medical conditions on both sides of the family, as well as any prior deaths of children and causes when known. Prior deaths of children could suggest a genetic or medical problem that should be addressed.

It is often the case with older children and adolescents that symptoms of illness do not appear prior to the death. The considerations as discussed should be applied to every case as appropriate for the age of the decedent. The autopsy may provide an immediate cause in cases of an existing condition or acute illness.

The good news is that the information gathered should provide the relevant medical history necessary for the investigation. Certainly not every case will require every medical record. Each case will be different. The bad news is that it still may not provide any answers. Negative circumstances and negative medical history lead us to the scene and environment for possible clues.

Environment

Anytime we go into someone else's home it is a learning experience. Much can be gained by observing and absorbing the environment. This is especially true when a child lives in that environment. Whether it is a gut feeling or trained eye, an investigator develops impressions and judgments about how a child lives and is taken care of in that setting. As already indicated, when dealing with natural deaths, often the scene and environment will be negative. That is negative in the sense that nothing blatant may stand out as far as evidence. The home may look similar to his or her own, or be dangerously unkempt. While what the investigator sees is important, what is not seen can be just as significant. Where is the child "stuff"? Stuff should be present where a child lives! "Stuff" can be defined as:

- Basic necessities (food, formula, bottles, diapers, etc.).
- Clothing (clean, dirty, folded, thrown in floor).
- Toys (from blocks to play stations, anything age appropriate).

- Age appropriate medicines (OTC and prescription).

Are the basic needs of the child being met? Are the developmental needs of the child being met? A child can die a natural death but live in a neglectful environment. One necessarily has nothing to do with the other. Remember also that what is observed, while seemingly benign at the time, now has a different significance due to the death.

Bear in mind, at the time of the death, nothing is known. The determination of manner as natural could take several months so every aspect of the environment is important to the investigation. Begin with the immediate environment, where the decedent is actually found and expand to cover the entire living and social environment. Remember Rule #2 when dealing with children: *they do not live in a vacuum*. They exist in a system and that entire system must be taken into account during the course of an investigation.

The following environmental considerations must be taken into account:

- Location of death — Home, other residence, daycare, hospital, other location.
- General impressions — Cleanliness, organization, etc.
- Identify "stuff" — There are no standards for what to collect, but a general rule is to collect anything related to the immediate environment at a minimum (bottles, bedding, clothing, etc.).
- Positions — How was the infant placed (face up, face down, face to side) or how did the child lie down to go to sleep, how were they found? Very important with infants under three months of age that may not have head control. Document if the position placed is the position the child typically sleeps in (i.e., always sleeps on back, but placed on stomach).
- Sleeping arrangements — It is critical to document specifics with infants co-sleeping with siblings and adults in order to rule out accidental asphyxiation. Specifically detail the following:
  ○ Number of people in the bed, adults and children
  ○ Positions in the bed (child in between adults, beside sib, etc.)
  ○ Height and weight of all in the bed (just describing them as large is not sufficient)

- Sleep location — Bed, crib, couch, floor, etc. Provide a description of the bedding, pillows, extraneous bedding, type of material, etc.
- Last meal — Document when given, by whom, what was it, how was it given (infants breast or bottle fed), any vomit present.
- Smoking and/or alcohol use in home — Who uses what, how often and how much. If an infant case, did the mother smoke during pregnancy?
- Temperature in home — Document the ambient temperature in the room where the child was found, document the type of heating system (electric, gas, wood stove, none), and detail the location of the heat source in relation to where the child was found.
- Medications — Document *all* medications in the home and to whom they belong, over-the-counter (OTC) and prescription (legal and illegal!). It is also important to note what meds mother takes if she was breastfeeding.

Again, it will be important to apply these considerations appropriately given the age of the decedent. The location of the death, positions of the decedent, meals, activities and medications may prove more crucial for older children and adolescents than other factors.

Now let's examine the significance of these considerations. The location of the death is important for several reasons. First, ensure the initial location is the only location (*scene*) related to the death. In most cases, the hospital will be a secondary location when the child is transported. If both scenes are not secured, information is lost. Second, when a child dies in a licensed facility, such as a residential home, day care center, or day care home, specific licensing and regulatory agencies will be involved in the investigation. Last, general impressions of the scene are important; however, beware of judgments. People live differently, perhaps because of lack of resources, wealth of resources, culture, or choice. Regardless of the circumstances, judgments and assumptions should be left at the door. Consciously or subconsciously, those biases guide thinking and often lead to details getting glanced over or not gathered.

The good, the bad and the ugly should all be documented and taken into consideration.

The position at the time of death and at the time they went to sleep is more pertinent to the children under one year of age. It is crucial to understand that an asphyxial death and Sudden Infant Death Syndrome can look identical at autopsy, meaning a negative autopsy. When dealing with infants less than one year of age, positional asphyxia and overlay must be ruled out in order to rule manner as natural. So consider first of all, does the infant have head control yet? Typically, most infants gain sufficient head control around three months. Thus, a face down position for infants found unresponsive under that age becomes an important investigative detail. Note however that plenty of infants do sleep face down and prefer sleeping face down, and do not suffocate.

The location the child was sleeping is important in order to eliminate asphyxiation, but also to rule in other possibilities. For example, in older children to adolescents, they are last seen to be in bed but are found on the bedroom or bathroom floor. Did they fall out of bed, or attempt to get to the bathroom, etc.? Perhaps a seizure or illness occurred during the night. The bottom line is to determine if the location found is different than the location placed and why.

The last meal eaten should be documented regardless of age. In instances where sickness or vomiting is part of the history it may be necessary to eliminate allergic reactions, poisoning, or aspiration. With infants, meals go hand-in-hand with sleeping and are a typical part of the initial history. It is important to document whether the baby was breast or bottle fed, when they last ate, who fed the baby, and how much was eaten.

Last, but most importantly, document the medications in the home. That is *all* medications (OTC and prescription) belonging to caregivers, other adults in the home, siblings, and the decedent. It is important to know what types of drugs are present in the home which are not part of the standard toxicological analysis at autopsy so that the appropriate analyses can be performed. Investigators should not limit questions regarding medications to just the immediate caregivers if other adults are present in the home. Some adults think that a small amount of their medication is appropriate to give to a child or infant, not knowing the medication could contain various components toxic to children.

Sudden Infant Death Syndrome

SIDS is an acronym that essentially means the medical community has no explanation for what caused the death. Thus it is a diagnosis of exclusion because there is nothing left to explain the death. SIDS has been around for decades, and most likely prior to that without a label. Theories have come and gone, yet most agree on several areas:

1) It is a respiratory issue. Whatever is occurring, call it disease or condition if you prefer, is related to the respiratory system in these young infants. They go to sleep and they do not wake up. Whether it is exclusively respiratory, what other systems are involved and to what extent are still being studied. There is no known cause. 2) Common findings exist at autopsy, such as petechial hemorrhages on the lung and thymus gland surfaces, and pulmonary edema and congestion. Unfortunately the findings do not provide a cause of death. 3) It is unpredictable. While risk factors have been identified, it is impossible to predict if an infant will succumb to SIDS. 4) It is unpreventable. It is understood that what is occurring systemically can not be interrupted.

Babies and SIDS are complicated. While SIDS is neither predictable nor preventable, there are identified risk factors associated with the diagnosis. Risk factors for SIDS include (but are not limited to) the following:

- Sex — more male infants die from SIDS than females
- Race — more minority infants die from SIDS
- Age — officially can be diagnosed from birth to one year, peak age range is 2–4 months of age
- Sleep Position — Risk is increased when infants that typically sleep supine are placed prone. Recommended practice is on the back to sleep.

- Sleeping arrangements—Co-sleeping increases the risk
- **Breast feeding—Note that breastfed infants are at a lesser risk for SIDS.

The remaining considerations include smoking/alcohol use, overheating, and medications. As smoking is the leading risk for SIDS, it is important to document use in the home as well as prenatal use by the mother. With regards to alcohol, document usage in the home, and specifically any usage suspected or confirmed in the time frame surrounding the death. If it is suspected that caregivers are under the influence of drugs or alcohol at the time of the death, secure blood samples for toxicological analysis. In the immediate location where the child was found, document the temperature of the room as accurately as possible, as well as the overall temperature of the house. Much attention has been paid to the issue of overheating in babies.

As their systems are quite immature and developing, they do not possess the ability to thermo-regulate, so their core body temperatures can rise too high. Theories suggest they overheat causing their systems to essentially shut down. How many times have you seen young infants with sweaty heads, red faces and clammy skin, after of course removing the two layers and cute baby cap? Babies are radiators, but for some reason caregivers like to wrap them in layers. Investigators should document the type of heating in the environment, and specifically, where the heat source is in relation to where the child was found. For example, is the crib situated over the heat vent, or is the kerosene heater located beside the mattress on the floor?

Before the diagnosis of SIDS can be attributed to a death, the American Academy of Pediatrics[1] requires three areas of investigation to be completed. First is a negative autopsy, including negative toxicology, histology, and any other tests. Second is the medical

---

1. Willinger M, James LS, Catz C. Defining the sudden infant death syndrome (SIDS): deliberations of an expert panel convened by the National Institute of Child Health and Human Development. *Pediatr Pathol.* 1991;11:677–684.

history, all of which should be negative. And last, a scene investigation is conducted and is negative. Scene investigations are often compromised due to a lack of notification, depending on who is responsible for conducting the scene investigation. In some jurisdictions medical examiners, coroners or death investigators perform that function. In areas where law enforcement conducts the scene, they can be hampered by the lack of notification. When a death "looks" natural, they may not automatically be notified of the death.

Remember this key rule with regards to Sudden Infant Death Syndrome:

> An investigator will never in his or her career *ever* conduct a SIDS investigation. Period. What he or she *will* do is conduct a thorough and complete death investigation of an infant under the age of one year that following a negative autopsy, review of the medical history and scene investigation is determined to be the result of SIDS.

Read that rule twice so it sinks in! Refer to Rule #1 in the introduction. No death or decedent "looks" natural. Dead children look like dead children. Physicians and nurses at hospitals are not qualified to make the diagnosis of SIDS. When children present to hospitals and are pronounced, they are often not worked up clinically. Thus, no x-rays, scans or diagnostics are performed. It is not the role of physicians or nurses to determine cause or manner of death. All that can be said with any medical certainty is that the child is deceased. With no autopsy and no investigation at that time, there is no diagnosis. The determination of SIDS can take months. While the physical autopsy usually takes less than one hour, the additional testing can take much longer.

Understand that natural deaths can and will occur with a child or infant in bed with a caregiver(s). However, co-sleeping remains a risk factor for both SIDS and asphyxiation. So again, asphyxiation must be ruled out in a co-sleeping arrangement in order to rule SIDS in as the cause of death. We will look at additional investigative details with regards to co-sleeping in chapter five.

This text was originally written in 2007. While the diagnosis of SIDS still exists, significant changes have occurred and are continuing to occur with regards to how infant deaths are ruled across the country. There seems to be a never ending barrage of new acronyms being assigned to these cases. Unfortunately, the new acronyms do not provide an anatomical cause of death, and still result in inconsistent applications to final determinations of both cause and manner of death. We will take a closer look at these terms, what they mean, and the implications of their use.

SIDS — Sudden Infant Death Syndrome

This diagnosis has never been without controversy. Bear in mind it is defined by the American Academy of Pediatrics, so there is no true pathological definition, hence it has always been subject to the leanings of the individual pathologist. The arbitrary age limit has also been a point of contention for some as well, arguing that it should be extended to include babies up to eighteen months of age. As with many things in this field, there are believers, naysayers, and fence riders. The end result is the same — Inconsistency.

SUDI — Sudden Unexplained/Unexpected Death in Infancy

This term refers to infant deaths that may meet the criteria for SIDS, but a thorough investigation reveals potential contributory causes or risk factors. Unsafe sleeping conditions without proof of asphyxiation, and autopsy findings that did not specifically cause the death are examples of contributing factors.

SUID — Sudden Unexplained Infant Death

This term can be used interchangeably with SIDS or it can be used to describe cases with contributing but not causative factors. The National Association of Medical Examiners has produced a white paper outlining their recommendations for using this term and investigative guidelines. The manner of death can be either Natural or Undetermined, however, Undetermined is recommended in cases where the true nature of the death is not known.

Now doesn't that make sense? So now instead of having one orig-inal acronym that did not explain how an infant died, we have two more which tell us even less. So let's cut to the chase here. Every in-fant death is sudden, unexpected and initially unexplained, mean-ing they ALL begin as SUID. It is only after the investigative process has been completed that it becomes something more definitive, and can be ruled accident, homicide, or natural. When the cause remains inconclusive, it is an undetermined death. No one wants answers in these cases more than the families. They crave honest ex-planations and they deserve nothing less. If the cause can not be de-termined, then that is what should be communicated. Dressing rulings up with contrived terms serves no purpose. The end result is still the same: Inconsistent applications of terms for cause and in-consistent manners of death.

Investigators are in the most likely position of interfacing with families and I encourage them to use "undetermined" in place of SUID or SUDI. That is exactly what they mean. Undetermined means there may have been either too much information or too little in-formation to be able to say precisely what caused the child's death. Defer families to the pathologist if they want clarification. The in-vestigations required for these deaths are all the same. They are deaths of infants which require a great amount of detail so they all get in-vestigated the same thorough way. Our job is to investigate and pro-vide the pathologist with the most accurate information possible.

Summary

Bear in mind many of the natural deaths investigated will have gross pathological findings at autopsy that will perhaps answer all questions, or guide the direction of the investigation. Regardless of age, by collecting all the investigative details we have discussed, the necessary information will be available to the pathologists to make the appropriate determinations in a natural death. Most im-portantly, an appropriate investigation can reveal details sugges-tive of a different manner. Remember the rules, drop your assumptions, and never think that a detail is unimportant.

Case Examples

The following examples provide a brief initial history, similar to what is relayed to medical examiners, coroners and pathologist upon initial report. Take each history and design an inquiry, develop questions for the pathologist and all potentially involved agencies, and list possible causes of death. Readers can check their inquiries against the full analysis provided in Appendix A.

1) 18 month old found deceased in crib at home. Child has history of mental retardation. Scene noted to be filthy with what appears to be vomit in the crib. One other sibling in home.
2) 17 year old male found dead in bed at home. No past medical history.
3) 15 year old male had seizure at school and later died. Illegal drugs found in his pocket.
4) 10 year old with a history of being sick within the past 36 hours prior to death. Found dead in bed at home.

Investigation to Do List

❑ Document history and circumstances
❑ Document all persons in home and relationship to decedent
❑ Document who was with child, who found child, who was supervising child
❑ Document location of death
❑ Document activities prior to and leading up to the death
❑ Establish timeline for activities and/or symptoms in previous 24–72 hours
❑ Document any observed signs and symptoms of illness preceding the death
❑ Document time last seen alive (LSA) and activity at that time
❑ Document all positions (when placed, when last seen, when found)

- ❑ Document past medical history (birth, recent medical history or illness, hospitalizations, pregnancy and prenatal)
- ❑ Document any relevant family medical history
- ❑ Description of sleeping location
- ❑ Crib exam (when applicable)
- ❑ Document details of co-sleeping arrangements
- ❑ Document last meal and time eaten
- ❑ In cases involving infants under one year of age document smoking, ambient temperatures, heating sources, types of pets
- ❑ Body description (marks, rigor, lividity, external trauma)
- ❑ Scene description
- ❑ Document any fluids observed at scene
- ❑ Document resuscitative efforts
- ❑ Obtain appropriate reconstructions
- ❑ Document all medications in home
- ❑ Document drug and alcohol use in home
- ❑ Document applicable outside agency involvement and histories
- ❑ Take photographs and/or draw scene diagrams and share with pathologist

CHAPTER 5

ACCIDENT

*Life is filled with ups and downs but most of the time I'm
going sideways.*

—Leslie, age 11

A five-year-old female is reported missing by caregiver
at approximately 1:30 p.m. Decedent located by father
in neighbor's pool at approximately 2:15 p.m. EMS
called, child pronounced at scene.

While any child death is tragic, accidental deaths of children
carry their own sense of tragedy because so many are preventable.
Children are not responsible for themselves, and teenagers still
require guidance. That is why it is called 'parenting' and 'care
giving.' Thus, an important investigative consideration with accidental death investigations is accountability. What exactly occurred? Who is responsible (i.e., accountable) for the child? What
were the circumstances leading up to the death? Is someone accountable for those circumstances? What, if any, culpability exists?

It is not possible to discuss every way accidental deaths occur.
We will explore the typical types of accidental deaths and considerations for each. In contrast to natural deaths where much is
unknown at the beginning, circumstances are generally known
and straightforward in the majority of accidental deaths. Investigative considerations will vary from case to case and guide the
course of the overall investigation. We will begin with the most
common means of accidental death in children, motor vehicle
crashes.

Motor Vehicle Crashes

Motor vehicle crashes can apply to several different mechanisms. Children in vehicles that crash, children as pedestrians, children on bicycles, all-terrain vehicles, children on anything with wheels, can all fall under this category. Children as passengers in vehicles will certainly comprise the highest numbers of fatalities across all age ranges.

With children as passengers in motor vehicle crashes, the crash report completed by law enforcement will be the most important investigative piece of information. The specific details relevant to a child death investigation involving a motor vehicle include but are not limited to restraint, condition of driver, speed, driver error, and applicable charges, and will be included in this report regardless of age. With younger children and infants, the most sought after detail will be restraint. Infants must be in car seats, but be sure to confirm that the carrier was actually attached to the car seat and attached properly. Infants not secured are generally considered unrestrained passengers. As children age and grow, statutes will dictate the use of larger seats and booster seats by either age, weight or both. Investigative considerations for children as drivers will include condition of driver, speed, various driver errors and seat belt usage. States have adopted different restrictive programs through which new drivers obtain their driver's license. Examples include limiting the times they can drive (no night driving), having an adult present in the car, no passengers, and a longer period of restricted driving.

Children struck by vehicles, either as pedestrians or riding near moving vehicles, involve supervision and/or neglect as the critical investigative consideration. Specific questions to be answered are:

- What were the circumstances? Who was where, when and what were they doing?
- Who was watching the child at the time?
- How did the child get in the position to be struck?

In addition to gathering these details, a timeline should be created documenting specific actions at specific times by all involved.

Combined, this information will provide precise details as to how the accident occurred, whether or not an aspect of neglect was involved, and if enough evidence exists for charging someone in the death. From a medicolegal perspective, these details provide a pathologist necessary information to compare to the autopsy findings in making a final determination of cause and manner of death. Examples of deaths related to motor vehicles cover the spectrum. There will certainly be those cases that are tragic and unavoidable (child darting out between parked cars), those involving the stereotypical "minute" of looking away (child wanders out of yard), and those that are so neglectful they result in criminal charges (unsupervised child playing in road). Investigative success will be in the details.

All terrain vehicles (ATV) are popular for both recreation and work related activities. ATV deaths involving children comprise a subset of motor vehicle deaths, and involve children as both passengers and drivers. They are unique in that they often occur on private property, complicating legal and regulatory issues. Investigative considerations will focus on either safety or regulatory issues and operational laws, or supervision of the child. Each state is different in the approach to these deaths. Investigators should examine state statutes for legislation pertaining to the operation of ATVs. Typically, ATV legislation focuses on the following:

- Helmets and safety equipment
- Age of driver
- Size of engine and age of driver—smaller ATVs for smaller drivers
- Licensing and safety courses
- Passengers—a critical issue when the above are all followed

Pathologically, the injuries will be consistent with the history. There may be cases where the child is found after the accident occurred so what actually caused the accident is unknown. While helmets reduce risk, also consider that many of these deaths involve other types of trauma. When an adult-sized ATV flips over backwards onto a small ten-year-old driver, crushing injuries or perhaps asphyxiation may occur. The two-year-old situated in front of the adult driver gets ejected or run over when the ATV hits a bump, suffering blunt force trauma or internal injuries. Circumstances will vary as will consequences. Websites for manufacturers and dealers often have operational and safety guidelines posted.

Asphyxiation

The mechanisms by which accidental asphyxiations occur are varied. We will examine each and discuss the investigative considerations as they apply.

Choking is a common form of asphyxiation in younger children and infants, though it can occur across all ages. Infants and toddlers learn by tasting their environment. Thus, anything small enough to fit in the mouth is fair game. Vigilance is the rule for caregivers. Typical histories in these cases will indicate a witnessed event. In rare cases, neglect may be a factor and will likely be indicated in the initial statements and scene investigation. Aspiration can also occur but will be determined microscopically by a pathologist. Documentation of vomiting at the scene is important, but does not necessarily imply aspiration.

Entrapment involves a child getting into an object, structure or environment in which they can not breathe or escape. These deaths will occur across all ages. Infants that are beginning to pull up and cruise suffer from the "Top Heavy Syndrome," carrying a significant percentage of their body weight on their shoulders. Unfortunately, this makes them vulnerable to flipping. The exploratory nature of children can lead them into situations not anticipated. Examples of these deaths can include children becoming trapped in containers with lids, appliances, vehicles and trunks, and tunnels.

Ligature strangulations involve an object that encircles the child's neck in some fashion. The stereotypical example would be the blind cord hanging in the crib and the child is discovered entangled. Certainly ropes, strings, straps, and cords of every kind could be potential hazards so the environment plays a critical role. Again, these deaths span the age range and lack of supervision may be an investigative consideration depending on circumstances. With hanging deaths, there are two scenarios that will need to be carefully investigated as they are accidental deaths, but can look like suicides. The first will be autoerotic asphyxiation. These deaths are recognizable by indicators such as the mechanisms in place, some type of release mechanism, pornography, nude or partially nude body, and possibly a video camera. Investigators may only find indicators of masturbatory sexual activity with no other indicators, or no indicators at all. It is possible to engage in the behavior for fantasy purposes and not sexual gratification. That leads into the second scenario. Deaths are increasingly being observed in children from the "hanging game" or "space monkey." It is simply a variation of self-asphyxiation without the sexual or fantasy overtones. Kids set up a situation to initiate asphyxiation and release at the right moment to *cheat* death. What these decedents fail to take into account is how quickly one becomes disoriented without sufficient oxygen to the brain. While he or she may have created a "foolproof" release mechanism, disorientation will effectively cancel that out, resulting in the inability to reverse the situation and ultimately death. The purpose behind these activities is *not* to die, thus the manner attributed to them is accidental.

Mechanical asphyxiation, sometimes referred to as traumatic asphyxiation, involves a mechanism of some sort compressing the decedent in such a way that they can not breathe, similar to entrapment deaths without the containment aspect. For example, an 11 year-old girl riding her horse and it slips. While initially only pinning her legs, as the horse struggles to stand it wallows on top of her causing crushing injuries to the chest, preventing her from breathing. Similar histories reveal some type of pinning or restraint between and under equipment. These are often witnessed or the circumstances are clear as first responders arrive on the scene to assist the victim.

The preceding types of asphyxial deaths can occur at any age. From an investigative perspective, circumstances may be straight forward or possibly witnessed. Special consideration will be given to those cases not witnessed, involving lack of supervision, or unknown circumstances. Investigative inquires will focus on documenting mechanisms, supervision, histories and circumstances. The remaining three types of accidental asphyxiations that will be covered focus on infants under one year of age and have significant investigative considerations. The most important consideration being the scene and investigative details gathered. The autopsy results in asphyxiations can be negative, just as in a SIDS death. Thus, the pathologist has only the body to consider initially, with negative findings to provide any specific details related to cause and manner. The pathologist will be relying on the investigation to put the death into context and make the appropriate determinations.

Deaths by overlay are categorized by a history of co-sleeping and indicators that at some point the infant was either rolled on, laid on, or whose breathing was compromised by a co-sleeper in some way. These deaths commonly occur under one year of age. The important rule for investigating overlay deaths is to *never* ask a caregiver if he or she rolled over on the child. What do you think their response would be? "Of course not," "I would never," "How could you suggest," "I would wake up if…." It is a question that can quickly halt effective gathering of critical details. It is possible to get specific information regarding a person's sleeping behaviors by asking other types of questions. Consider asking the following types of questions: are they light or heavy sleepers? Do they toss and turn frequently? Do the covers become disheveled or stay neat during the night? Has the child been put in the bed on previous occasions without them being aware? Do they regularly co-sleep with the infant? Do they always hear the child at night or provide primary care during the night? The following details should *always* be gathered in any case of a history involving co-sleeping with an infant:

- Number of persons in the bed—While it may seem like an unimportant detail, when you count adults and children the total could reach four to six easily.
- Positions of those in the bed—Document specifically where each person was in the bed initially and when they awoke. For example, it is a common practice to place infants between a caregiver and the wall to keep them from falling out of the bed. Document where each person was sleeping in the bed in relation to the decedent.

- Size of co-sleepers—Document the height and weight of all co-sleepers. The difference between a ninety pound mother sleeping on a couch with her infant and a two hundred fifty pound father sleeping on the same couch with an infant can be significant.
- Location—Document the exact location (bed, couch, etc) and the size (couch width, double bed, twin).
- Evidence of drug or alcohol use at the time—Investigators should make every attempt to obtain proof of intoxication.
- Presence of fluids on individuals, bedding, decedent, clothing, sleep location.

As discussed previously, co-sleeping becomes a significant investigative consideration when trying to distinguish between SIDS and asphyxiation. Some professionals believe co-sleeping in and of itself cancels out a diagnosis of SIDS, resulting in a determination of either undetermined or accidental as the manner of death. Opinions aside, co-sleeping as well as sleeping prone, do not automatically mean asphyxiation. If that were true, a significant percentage of us would not be alive as we were surely placed in bed on our bellies and slept with our parents as babies. Ask your own mother and see how she put you to bed. No detail is unimportant when co-sleeping is part of the history in a death.

Positional asphyxias typically occur between the ages of birth to two years. Infants gain head control around the age of three months. Thus, infants under three months of age are at a higher risk when placed prone, whether that is in a bed, crib or on a caregiver's chest. They either get into or are placed in a position in which they can not raise their head to breathe. Tummy playtime for infants is critical to their developmental progress, allowing them to utilize and strengthen the neck muscles. However, any sleep periods should have infants face up, especially prior to mastering head control. Investigative considerations will include the following:

- Position placed—Remember to document if this is the typical position for this child.

- Position found—Document whether the child can independently get into this position.
- LSA (Last Seen Alive)—This must be an activity or awake time, unless the person physically checks the child and can say the child was still breathing but sleeping.
- Developmental abilities—Find out from the caregiver what the child is capable of developmentally (rolling over, front to back, back to front, sitting up, head control, etc).

Another common form of positional asphyxiation is wedging. Typical histories can include infants becoming wedged between crib rails and mattresses, between beds and walls, sofa cushions, or rolling off of beds into head down positions. It is important to note that wedging can occur in a co-sleeping situation without overlay. It will be important to make that distinction in an investigation. Investigative considerations will include the following:

- Sleeping arrangements
- Crib exams—Inspect for missing, stripped, or malfunctioning hardware, and that the mattress fits the crib. If there is any 'give' at all in the sides, or gaps between mattress and rail, it is a potentially deadly environment.
- Last Seen Alive
- Positions
- Developmental abilities
- Neglect
- Type of sleeping surface and description

The last category of accidental asphyxiation is smothering. This involves a child or infants face being occluded by an object or material. Examples could include excessive bedding, sheets or blankets around the head or face, or faces in contact with plastic in varying ways. Investigative details will be critical in order to provide the pathologist with the complete context so that the appropriate determinations of cause and manner can be made. The body evidence (or lack of) and a vague description of a child being face down will not be sufficient. Investigative considerations will again include positions, LSA, and developmental abilities, but will also extend to the sleeping environment itself. Specifically, provide photos of the bedding, descriptions of the bedding (cotton, wool, silk), thickness of the bedding, and how tight or loose (if wrapped). This information should be provided to the pathologist at the time of the autopsy or as soon as possible afterwards. Depending on physical findings, the scene and investigative details may be the determining factors for cause and manner of death.

Drowning

Regardless of geographic location, drowning deaths demonstrate similar trends. These trends tend to show the ages at which certain types of drowning deaths occur and the location of the drowning. Tub deaths exemplify this trend, occurring typically with infants and toddlers. It takes only "a minute and an inch." Drowning deaths can however occur anywhere, from buckets to pools, ponds, creeks, and fish ponds. Investigative considerations will focus primarily on supervision and neglect, activity at the time, swimming ability, and age of the child.

Pool deaths can occur at any age but for different reasons. There is a tendency towards higher numbers in the 0–4 year age range. There are three key reasons for this trend.

- Lack of supervision—These histories typically involve a child wandering away from a caregiver or an adult only turning their back for "a minute."
- Combination of curiosity and complete lack of fear—During this age range, children typically have only positive associations with water.
- They have not yet learned to swim—Prevention strategies commonly involve encouraging swim lessons for all ages.

Pool deaths in older children and teenagers occur more often for reasons related to swimming ability and behavior. They may overestimate their abilities, combine swimming and alcohol or attempt to swim in an unfamiliar environment. Occasionally a drowning death can occur due to an existing condition such as a seizure disorder.

Natural bodies of water can involve activities other than swimming, such as boating, canoeing, fishing and riding recreational water toys. The trend tends towards older children drowning in these circumstances. Depending on the history, a focus of these investigations will be determining if operational laws were broken, such as age and use of floatation devices.

Depending on the age of the child and the circumstances, the following investigative considerations should be explored:

- Supervision—Is supervision an issue and does it meet the criteria for neglect?
- Pools—Codes will typically dictate the types of pools that can be installed, fencing requirements, and recommended safety equipment. Fences are commonly required to be either three or four-sided, and codes may specify the types of gates or locks that must be installed. Common types of safety equipment recommended include alarm systems and covers.
- Operational laws—Age of operation of recreational water crafts and use of life jackets will vary across jurisdictions and types of water.
- Swimming ability—If it can be confirmed that they could swim, examine what other factors could have contributed to the death.
- History—Is there a pattern of neglect or lack of supervision in the child or family history?

Drowning deaths can occur wherever water is present. The investigative considerations will vary with the circumstances and age of the child. The important thing to remember is that these deaths are often ruled primarily on circumstances. Investigators should not rely on the autopsy to provide all of the answers.

Guns

I often pose the following question to students, "How many of you were raised in homes with guns?" Overwhelmingly, the majority will raise their hands. I then ask, "What kept you alive?" Without hesitation, the response is consistently "I knew better" or something to that effect. Whether a result of teaching rules, or instilling the fear of God, it worked. Accidental shooting deaths of children are troubling because they are often self-inflicted or are child-on-child acts. Hunting season inevitably results in a few cases each year as well. These deaths all share common denominators, lack of education and safety, lack of supervision, and accessibility. Gun related laws serve a purpose and do prevent deaths; however, that lack of education and safety can be what gets a child killed even if the law is followed to the letter. Investigators will often find that aspect missing. These children often have no knowledge that guns are dangerous. Thus, it is not a gun control issue; it is a common sense issue. Even when the safety aspect is covered, unsupervised children with access to guns is never an appropriate combination.

Investigative considerations will be affected by state laws governing ownership and storage of guns. First and foremost, supervision will be crucial, particularly in the younger ages. Second, reconstructions and specific accounts of what occurred will be necessary to match with the autopsy findings. Last, establish type, ownership, and storage of the weapon and whether laws pertaining to each were broken. It is also critical to document any use of guns by the decedent and familiarity with the weapon used. Scene considerations should also include how the child gained access to the weapon, both when properly and improperly stored.

Fire

Fire deaths are especially tragic both in the totality of the loss, and the loss of life, commonly more than one in a single fire. Typically, these fires involve mechanical or electrical malfunctions, or human error. Investigative details regarding cause and origin can be obtained from the local fire marshal or other investigative agency. Those reports should contain the details pertinent to the death investigation and include other relevant information about use of fire alarms and other preventive measures. Special consideration is given to cases involving children left unattended at the time of the fire. Children left alone will attempt to take care of themselves by cooking, lighting things, or turning on heat sources. It should be determined whether neglect was a factor related to the cause of the fire and subsequent death. Autopsy findings should confirm if the child or children succumbed to smoke inhalation or thermal injuries. Investigative considerations will include establishing cause and origin of the fire, safety mechanisms in place, type of structure, and number of deaths involved.

Drugs

Accidental overdoses span the age range of children and involve a multitude of drugs and medications. Most commonly, the toxicity cases of younger children and infants involve a child getting into an accessible bottle or medicine, not to exclude illegal drugs lying out in the open. Another situation that arises is when an adult gives a child a small amount of his or her medication thinking a small amount will be sufficient. Unfortunately, it could be sufficiently toxic. In any toxicity case, it is critical that *all* adults in a household, whether a caregiver or not, be questioned about his or her medications. Be sure to gather information on all medicines, prescription and over the counter, which may be in the household. It may be that someone other than the parent gave a dose to the child. These cases may not involve intent or malice, but certainly neglect should be considered. Scenes and histories may reveal indicators that the toxin is an illegal drug. Special consideration should be given to how the toxin got into the child's system. In cases of infants, document if the mother breast or bottle fed the baby.

As we move into the deaths of older children and adolescents, we embark on an experimental journey. Kids can, will and do try anything to see how it will make them feel. Whether they prefer to pop it, drink it, snort it, huff it, or free-base, there is a medication or chemical available. If not readily available, they know where to get it, perhaps even their own house. Medications typically thought of for adults are being prescribed more to young people, making it accessible through friends.

Investigative considerations will vary by age but will include the following:

- Supervision or neglect — A thorough scene investigation should include full list of medications and drugs in house.
- Accessibility — How did they get the med/drug?
- Prescriptions — Who has them and are they legitimate?
- Drugs — If illegal drugs are involved, do they relate to the death and how?

The more common drugs observed in overdoses of adolescents tend to be prescription medications. Overdoses from oxycontin, hydrocodone, and methadone are common among adolescent ages, with combinations of these drugs mixed with alcohol and other recreational drugs also occurring. Investigative considerations should focus on the accessibility of the drugs. While the majority will likely come from within the household, there will be situations of medical professionals abusing their prescriptive powers. Locate the source and determine if the drugs were obtained illegally.

Falls

It is the rare case of a child that dies from an accidental fall. When it does occur, the injuries are consistent with the history and scene investigation. For example, falling thirty feet from bleachers at a stadium, falling off a bridge, or falling from a tree stand. Because falls are a common false history with homicides, any history with a fall should be thoroughly investigated, particularly in the younger ages. Reconstructions should be conducted when possible, and good communication should occur between the pathologist and law enforcement to ensure that the injuries, history and scene are consistent. Documentation should be gathered regarding the location of the fall, and to what surface they fell, if the fall was witnessed, and the distance fell.

Summary

Anything can happen. Investigations of accidental deaths are typically straight forward, with the focus being to confirm the circumstances with the final autopsy report and related agency histories. The complicating factors tend to be those deaths involving neglect and potential illegal activities that resulted in the death. A variety of agencies could be involved in these types of investigations and it will be critical to make sure all related information is shared. Remember, it can all boil down to accountability.

Case Examples

The following examples provide a brief initial history, similar to what is relayed to medical examiners, coroners and pathologist upon initial report. Take each history and design an inquiry, develop questions for the pathologist and all potentially involved agencies, and list possible causes of death. Readers can check their inquiries against the full analysis provided in Appendix A.

1) 17 year old male found by father slumped over with a belt around his neck, attached to the doorknob of his bedroom door. Deceased was partially clothed, adult magazine located beside body, no history of depression or stress. Parents in the home at the time.
2) 14 year old with past history for use of Zoloft and alcohol. School history significant for known drug usage. Found dead in bed at home.
3) 9 week old female found deceased in bed with parents.
4) 5 year old male reportedly shot in home by sibling. Others present include children aged 4 and 8 years. Parents at store at time of shooting.

Investigation to Do List

Drowning

- ❑ Document type of body of water
- ❑ Document activity at time
- ❑ If pool, above or below ground, fencing, codes, lifeguard on duty
- ❑ Document use of floatation devices
- ❑ Document swimming ability
- ❑ Document supervision

Gun

- ❑ Document ownership and storage
- ❑ Document type of gun
- ❑ Document activity at the time
- ❑ Document supervision
- ❑ Fire/Burns
- ❑ Document source and origin of fire
- ❑ Document safety devices, alarms, and safety plans
- ❑ Document location of decedent in residence

Falls

- ❑ Document location of fall and location found
- ❑ Document supervision
- ❑ Document activities at time of fall

Toxins

- ❑ Document type (medication, drug, other toxin, etc)
- ❑ Document access, how obtained, supervision
- ❑ Document the source

MVC

- ❑ Document if driver, passenger or pedestrian
- ❑ Document type of vehicle
- ❑ Document restraint use
- ❑ Document cause of wreck (speed, driver error, road conditions, etc)
- ❑ Document safety devices (helmet, airbags, car seats, etc)

Asphyxiation

- ❑ Document location found
- ❑ Document positions, original and when found
- ❑ Document mechanism
- ❑ Document body findings (rigor, lividity)

CHAPTER 6

SUICIDE

Children are apt to live up to what you believe of them.
—Lady Bird Johnson

The taking of one's own life. Difficult to imagine, even more so when the choice is made by a child. Investigators must cast a 'broad net' over these cases to capture the full psychosocial history surrounding the decedent, as well as to find any communicative intent made by the decedent. The ruling of suicide requires two elements, intention and self-infliction. While the autopsy findings and scene investigation should provide evidence of self-infliction, the critical component will be establishing the intent. The strongest of investigations will be built on a solid, thorough psychosocial and emotional history of the decedent.

We need to first be familiar with what to expect with these cases. Our focus will be method and means. While statistics show the most likely victims to be white adolescent males with a handgun, everything is variable. What matters most is the investigative approach, which will be dependent on the means, as well as the age of the victim.

Guns

Parents arrive home after church around 1:30 p.m. and find their 14-year-old son dead in his bedroom from an apparent gunshot wound. There is a .38 handgun beside the bed.

When the investigator arrives on the scene, it will most likely be disturbed, both by family and first responders. It will be critical to document the decedent and weapon as they were initially found. Determine the owner of the gun and where it was last known to be kept or stored. Establish what familiarity the decedent had with the weapon and guns in general. That particular information may be helpful in ruling out accidental circumstances. The autopsy findings, specifically trajectories and distance or range, should confirm whether the shot was self-inflicted. Other forensic evidence such as gunshot residue (GSR) tests can also aid in this determination. Cases involving Russian Roulette are considered suicide and may or may not be witnessed. Cases involving several witnesses and the decedent putting the weapon to their head and pulling the trigger require special consideration. These cases are considered suicide, but potentially could be ruled accidental depending on circumstances. It is critical to develop a full history of the decedent, alcohol use at the time, and obtain statements from each witness as to what exactly occurred. It is typical in these situations for witnesses to argue that it was an accidental shooting. The determination of suicide under these circumstances will require full communication between investigators and pathologists.

Hanging

> Parents arrive home after church around 1:30 p.m. and find their 14-year-old daughter hanging from her closet door in her bedroom.

The first inclination of caregivers is to cut the child down and call 911, resulting in scene alterations. It will be crucial for the investigator to document, reconstruct if at all possible, how the child was suspended or found, and document the mechanism and how it was tied or assembled. Investigators should understand that hangings are not about suspension but pressure on the neck so victims can be found sitting, slumped or supported in some manner.

Unfortunately, the autopsy will only confirm that asphyxiation is the cause of death. The manner will be determined by the circumstances and investigation. Scenes may indicate experimental or autoerotic behavior. It is critical in an investigation to rule these factors out in order to rule a death as suicide.

Drugs

> Parents arrive home after church around 1:30 p.m. and find their 14-year-old son unresponsive in his bedroom. A pill bottle is found under the desk by the bed.

The numbers for drug overdose suicides are typically lower than guns and hangings; however, they do present certain challenges. As with hangings, a determination must be made between intentional and experimental behavior. Without a thorough investigation, that determination may not be possible. Investigators must document all medications and drugs found near the decedent. It is important to also document all medications and drugs belonging to all individuals living in the home. While it is possible they obtained the medication or drug from outside the home, it is more likely it was already in the home. Toxicology results may indicate targeting behavior of one drug with high levels or various levels of several drugs. The later scenario could suggest experimentation without the totality of evidence from an investigation to put the results into perspective. It will be important to establish any and all known drug and/or alcohol use by the decedent prior to the death.

The Broad Net

Now that we have identified the *what*, we need to delve into the *why*. The *why* will establish the manner of death. So investigators must cast a broad net over everyone having contact or communication with the decedent in the recent past. This broad net should include but not be limited to the following:

- Family (direct and extended)—They may not be the best source of information given that they live with the decedent. They simply may not recognize behavior changes as high risk.
- Friends (regular and acquaintances)—They typically know more than they may let on.
- Boyfriends or girlfriends—This is a very important relationship for young people.
- Teachers—They are in the best position to identify academic patterns.
- Guidance counselors—They may recognize high risk behaviors.
- Coaches—They may be a confidant.
- School Resource Officers—They have an excellent perspective on the kids in the schools.

After identifying those needing to be questioned, investigators need to design the questions. The important rule of thumb for questioning individuals in a suicide investigation is this: investigators will be trying to obtain information from people that potentially have critical information to share, but do not know they have that information. Caregivers and others close to the decedent will not attribute the same significance to details that investigators find pivotal. Thus, what is asked and how it is asked will determine the quality of information obtained. The following areas of questioning should be considered and will vary by age of the victim and the circumstances:

- Any changes in daily habits—Eating, sleeping, daily routines, cleanliness, appearance.
- Any changes in behavior—New routines, new activities, dropping old activities or routines, loss of interest, risk-taking behaviors, personal appearance, clothing changes.
- Any changes in personality—While 'moody' is a relative term, look for mood changes or swings, irritability, outbursts, uncharacteristic moods.
- Any changes in academic behaviors—Drops in grades, attendance, loss of interest, loss of concentration or participation.

- Any family or social changes—Divorce, break-ups, remarriages, relocations, change in school, death of relative or friend.

Ideally, these lines of questioning will produce some indicators of suicidal tendencies. Every detail is important, regardless of what the person providing the information believes.

Reasons

Suicides occur for a variety of reasons, but often those reasons remain unknown. Investigators should avoid the depression trap, assuming that to be a factor in the case at the onset. Descriptors such as down, depressed, sad, may be provided in an investigation, but do not mean the child was clinically depressed. Depression should be classified as a factor in the death when documentation of a mental health history, diagnosis, treatment, and/or medications is provided. Without that documentation, investigators may be dealing with opinion or supposition. Other reasons will be present at the surface, not layers beneath. Investigators must recognize that what he or she believes is a non-issue can be catastrophic to a child's way of thinking. Common reasons include break-ups, fight with a parent, a discipline problem at school or home, bullying or being picked on, a bad grade, perception of failure, and the list goes on. Many of these deaths are the result of an impulsive act, arguably not an act that was thought through. Some deaths occur during or following a heated argument, some as an act to get back at someone, and others to escape. Investigators can not go back and obtain a reason, and it is unfair to speculate what that reason might have been without knowing all the facts. Investigators should gather all the information, give each case due consideration, and make the most appropriate conclusion given what is known. It must be understood that there will be cases where the best investigation possible will not yield a reason for why a child killed himself or herself.

Communication

In the ideal situation, the decedent leaves a note explaining why he or she chose to end his or her life. In reality, suicide notes are left in a small percentage of cases. Communication can however take many forms. Verbal communications could be direct statements, subtle comments, to phone messages. Written communications may include notes, emails, journals or other writings. Technology has introduced so many ways to communicate without having to directly speak to someone, so investigators should explore all electronic modes of communication, especially text messages for any indicators of intent. Thus, standard protocols should include the collection and examination of computers and other devices. The greatest downfall of investigators in child suicides is identifying these communications. The primarily reason is because investigators may not recognize communications for what they are. As adults, we all are terrible about underestimating children. Children are literal; they say what they mean and mean what they say. Adults are just not bright enough to get it most of the time. Communications are often more subtle the younger the age of the child (e.g., Mom is mad at me, they do not want me, I need to go away for awhile). Therefore, any subtlety could be important. The older the age of the victim, the more blatant the communication may become (e.g., You won't have to worry about me anymore, I hate myself and want to die, I hate you and will kill myself). Nothing is unimportant, so investigators should document any and all communications made by the decedent to other individuals, both recent and past, that may be relevant.

Guidelines

The following guidelines will ensure the most detailed information is gathered and considered so the appropriate manner of death can be assigned. These areas should be addressed completely in the death of any child under the age of 18 years suspected to be due to self-inflicted and/or intentional means. The final manner of death could hinge on any one of these details.

History—The history can be broken down into three components: Initial, Recent and Past. The relevance of each will vary from case to case.

Initial—This will be the reporter's version of what happened when they discovered the body. It is important to record as much detail as possible about what they saw PRIOR to altering the scene, which is typically what happens immediately upon finding the decedent. Gather the following details:

What exactly did they see?

Did the decedent say or do anything prior to the death?

How were they dressed? Did the reporter redress the victim?

What did the reporter touch?

If hanging, how did they get them down?

If a gun death, where was the gun located? How was it accessed?

Did they alter or remove anything from the immediate scene?

Recent—This history encompasses the 24–48 hours prior to the death. So this history could potentially be 5–15 minutes prior to the death. The key here is identifying any possible triggers for the act. Everything becomes relevant even if the family does not believe so.

What occurred on that day that was upsetting, unusual, outside of the normal routine?

Did anything happen at school/game/home/etc?

Who did the decedent talk to when last seen/heard?

Any personal issues that can be identified?

Have there been any major family/school/personal changes within the last few days?

Make a specific timeline for the 24–48 hours prior to the death, marking any communications with anyone, and all typical routine activities and disruptions to the normal routine.

Past—Past history could potentially include any of the following (but not be limited to):

Family—death, divorce, illness, relocation, abuse, etc.

Psych/Mental Illness—with decedent or family member.

Sexual Abuse—any prior history of decedent as victim.

Circumstances Preceding Death
What was the decedent doing when last seen alive?
Did they say anything to anyone?
Did they talk/text to anyone on the phone?
Is there evidence of any other electronic communication?
What was the timeline for that day for the decedent?
Were there any unusual happenings or communications?

Scene Investigation
How was the decedent found (as detailed as possible)?
If hanging:
What were they hanging from?
What did they have around their neck?
How was it secured?
Any indications of a release mechanism?
Did they video themselves?
Any indicators of prior activity or usage present?
Any indicators present for auto-erotic asphyxiation?
If gun:
Was the decedent alone or with anyone at the time?
Who owns the gun?
How was the gun stored?
Document any familiarity/experience the decedent had with guns.

Psycho-Social History
Who to talk to—Remember that friends and families have significant information to contribute that they do/may not recognize as important. So designing questions and interview tactics to pull those details out of your conversations with them is crucial. Always keep in mind they do/may not want to believe it is suicide.

Activities—What was the decedent involved in? What was important to them?

Ideation—Has the decedent ever expressed suicidal ideation to anyone? Friends may have more relevant information about that than family members.

Substance Abuse History—Identify any history and what type of substances with the decedent and family members.

Medications—Document any medications, prescriptions and OTC, that the decedent was known to take or is suspected to have taken.

Communication
    Writings—Actual suicide notes are only written in about a third of the cases but they may have other writings that are valuable. Do they journal? Have they written down song lyrics or poems? Have they turned in school assignments that are questionable?
    Verbal—Have they verbalized to anyone? Even the most subtle communication could be important. Adults often overlook things children say.
    Other communication methods—Texting, blogging, online chat groups, and social networking sites are all targets to examine for communication.

Witnesses to asphyxial high activities—Often the asphyxial high activity originates in a group, then the victim starts doing it alone. Identifying a person that either witnessed the victim participating in the activity, doing the activity, or told them they were doing the activity can greatly enable the pathologist in making a determination of accident over suicide. Also important is determining if the decedent was looking at the behavior online, through search engines, Youtube, etc.

School History—What do teachers, counselors, nurses, SROs say about the decedent or know about the decedent? Any recent changes in class, grades, assignments, writings? Any history of trouble with classmates? Was the decedent involved in sports, injured, or failed to make a team?

Secure Electronics—Standard procedure must include collecting any and all electronic devices the decedent may have used to communicate, to include computers, cell phones, and any other mobile devices. Also access social media sites to see if acquaintances of the decedent have posted memorials.

Family History—Is there any relevant family history of substance abuse, mental illness, or psychiatric diagnoses, physical/sexual abuse? Has there ever been a suicide of a family member known to the decedent? Any recent death of a close family member?

History of Mental Illness—If there is a history, document the diagnosis and treatment. Also document any indications of prior suicide attempts by the decedent.

Summary

Suicide investigations are difficult for everyone. Circumstances may not provide obvious answers, the age of the child may hinder making conclusive determinations, and the family may strongly object to the ruling of suicide and insist it was accidental. Ideally, these investigations require the maximum amount of information and detail. For investigators, this means that the gathering of information, the type and how it is gathered, is the most important part of the process. With these cases, cause of death is not the issue. Determining whether the actions were self-inflicted and intentional make the difference in manner, and are the most important investigative pieces of the puzzle.

Case Examples

The following examples provide a brief initial history, similar to what is relayed to medical examiners, coroners and pathologist upon initial report. Take each history and design an inquiry, develop questions for the pathologist and all potentially involved agencies, and list possible causes of death. Readers can check their inquiries against the full analysis provided in Appendix A.

1) 12 year old male found hanging in his bedroom from a bedpost with a rope.

2) 14 year old female found in the garage by her mother with a gunshot wound to the head. Several notes recovered from the scene.

3) 15 year old male verbalized that he would kill himself before he moved. Younger sibling found him in room hanging from a closet bar.

Investigation to Do List

❑ Document decedent social and familial history
❑ Document any communications of intent
❑ Document activities preceding the death
❑ Document ownership and storage of gun, when applicable
❑ Document type of gun and location of gun at the scene
❑ Document original position of decedent in asphyxial cases
❑ Document mechanism used in asphyxial cases
❑ Document indicators of experimental behavior (suggestive of accidental asphyxia)
❑ When indicated, document all medications and drugs
❑ Document usage history of drugs and alcohol
❑ Conduct reconstructions whenever possible

CHAPTER 7

Homicide

Having children makes one no more a parent than having a piano makes you a pianist.

— Michael Levine

A 3-year-old female is found unresponsive on the couch. The father reports a history of vomiting after a fall onto the coffee table.

The means by which children are killed vary greatly. Most homicides of children are a result of frustration and lack of appropriate expectations of children, while others are calculated acts of violence. The methods and means observed in these murders are unique to children, thus investigators working these cases should have the relevant training and experience before being assigned to a child homicide. One rule will hold true for child homicides: the methods will change as the age of the child changes.

This trend can be attributed to a variety of factors including the size of the victims and perpetrators, the reaction by a caregiver to behaviors of a child, and accessibility to weapons. We will examine the different methods and means typically seen in child homicides beginning with the youngest victims. As with the preceding manners, it is important for investigators to be familiar with the trends in his or her jurisdiction.

Neonaticide

Surviving the first twenty-four hours of life is a tremendous accomplishment. It is during that time frame that many natural deaths occur, but also when infants are most likely to be killed by his or her own parent. Neonaticides are those murders occurring after the delivery of the infant, within the first twenty-four hours after the birth, typically following a concealed pregnancy. There is no stereotype for the mothers in these cases, they could be girls in middle school or mothers in their forties. All females of child bearing age are potential perpetrators in these cases. The two primary consistencies in these cases are the concealment of the pregnancy and the concealment of the birth itself.

There are several ways in which these deaths typically occur. Some of the infants are simply abandoned and left to die. Without proper care an infant will succumb to exposure, dehydration or other causes related to lack of care. Other mothers harm the child resulting in deaths from causes such as blunt force trauma and abusive head trauma. Asphyxiation is another common method involving typically either a manual suffocation, using her hands, or a containment suffocation where she places the child in a container, box, or wraps them in material. Drowning deaths can occur when the mother delivers into a toilet and the infant is left to drown in the water. While other means certainly can occur in these types of deaths, these are the most common observed.

The critical component to these cases is proving the child lived outside of the womb. There is no death, or homicide, if there is no life. The pathologist will ideally be able to determine that the infant took a breath, either through the preliminary exam or by the microscopic results. Depending on when the child is found, decomposition may occur and can result in that determination being inconclusive. The question of viability can arise which could possibly result in the death being classified as a fetal death.

Investigative considerations will include the following:

What is the history?

There may be no significant history when the infant is abandoned and found by strangers. The history in that case will be established through the investigation. A common history includes the birth being concealed but discovered by a family member or caregiver. Either the baby or evidence of the birth is found in the home. It should be established if anyone close to the mother knew she was pregnant. It will be important for the investigator to question the mother, if known, what she heard or observed after the birth. Did she hear the infant cry or make any noise, or were there any indications that child was alive? There are two trains of thought regarding her answers, that she may not have been in a state to recognize what was happening, or that she will incriminate herself with her responses that are contradicted by the autopsy.

Who is the mother?

Whatever else is discovered during the course of an investigation of an abandoned infant can be rendered useless if no mother is located. Without a known mother there is no known medical or birth history to review, no scene to speak of except for where the child was found, and ultimately no one to hold responsible for the death. Sometimes the women seek medical attention following the birth and treating physicians notify authorities. In other cases, a mother is never found. Often the media can be helpful and investigative leads develop as a result of the news coverage.

What are the final autopsy results?

Ideally the results will indicate that the child took a breath on its own after birth. It will be important to determine the gestational age of the child. When did the mother conceive and when did the birth take place? Some females may report not knowing they were actually pregnant, but most will be able to give enough information to establish when they became pregnant. These details will provide necessary information in the determination of viability which can be compared to autopsy findings. The pathologist will look for specific indicators, such as air in the lungs. A complication can arise if anyone attempted CPR on the infant at the time of discovery. Investigators need to document carefully, and include reconstructions, any attempts either by caregivers or medical personnel.

If the final results are inconclusive, varying charges can be explored related to the concealment of a birth or death.

If the results confirm homicide, what approach is taken?

The results are in: the cause of death is asphyxiation and the manner is homicide. In cases where it clearly was a deliberate act, the mother is old enough to understand her actions (by law and age) and strategically hid the pregnancy and disposed of the body, the approach is a standard homicide investigation. However, consider if the mother is 13 years old and delivers at home in the toilet. She leaves the baby for an undetermined amount of time, and tells no one else in the home. Her actions may have been deliberate, but the mother's age will weigh heavily in the approach to this case. There is no easy answer and the circumstances associated with these cases vary widely. All abandoned infant cases should be pursued aggressively. The critical aspects will be to determine that the child lived prior to being abandoned or killed, and locate the mother.

Many states now have legislation regarding the safe surrender of infants without fear of prosecution. While they vary in scope, several key elements serve as the foundation for these abandonment laws. First and foremost, it is an anonymous process. Second, there are provisions that do not protect those that may abuse or neglect an infant prior to surrender. Last, age limits are built into the laws so that one cannot surrender an infant over a certain age and remain immune to prosecution. The anonymity component is critical to the safety of the infant. Those professionals in a position of accepting an infant are encouraged to try to obtain medical history information from the caregiver, but should be clear that identifiable information is not needed. It is important to understand that there is no way to know how many of these cases are *not* discovered. While certain groups oppose the law, the facts are clear. The safe surrender of one infant in one town makes the legislation a success.

Abusive Head Trauma

While commonly referred to as Shaken Baby Syndrome or Shaken Impact Syndrome, Abusive Head Trauma is the terminology now used to describe the injuries typically seen in these types of homicides. There are varying opinions within the forensic pathology community about what actually causes these injuries. Some pathologists believe the injuries result from shaking alone, some believe them to be from blunt force trauma alone, while others believe a combination of forces on the brain leads to this particular constellation of injuries. Thus, the term Abusive Head Trauma (AHT) is used, describing the injuries regardless of how they occurred, and emphasizing that they are *non-accidental*.

The crux of the problem is that shaking and impact can look identical pathologically. Impacts can often be determined by physical indicators such as skull fractures or contusions, when present. However, these indicators may not be present in every case, but statements or confessions by caregivers can provide the specific mechanisms of injury. Pathologists will look for a combination of retinal hemorrhages, subdural and subarachnoid hemorrhages, and cerebral edema. These may occur in various combinations, but the presence of them at all, in combination with the history, may be a red flag. The pathologist and/or neuropathologist can explain what is present, what it indicates, and his or her opinion on the potential mechanisms of injury. Investigators must bear in mind the following when approaching these investigations:

- These cases are not 'cookie cutter' cases and can present differently, so approach each individually.
- If there is evidence of old injuries in conjunction with new be sure to get explanations for those as well.
- Aging of the injuries may be problematic in some cases, so the investigative details, timelines, and interview processes will assist the pathologist in ruling in or ruling out possible times of injury.

- Whenever possible, obtain preliminary autopsy results before engaging in the interview/interrogation stage.

All of the above can affect investigative approaches and outcomes as we will see as we take a closer look at investigative considerations. Now take a second look at the case example.

> A 3-year-old female is found unresponsive on the couch. The father reports a history of vomiting after a fall onto the coffee table.

Identify red flags

With this particular scenario, red flags would be a male caregiver, vague symptoms, and a common household accident. It is sad but true that typical perpetrators in these cases are mothers or a male caregiver. The symptoms reported initially can be vague (leg pain then unconsciousness) to nonexistent (they went limp). They simply will not coincide with the fact that the child is now crashing or already dead. Anytime there is an initial history of a fall, red flags should start flying. If children died from common household falls from short distances, most of us would not be alive. Feel free to confirm this with your own mother! There will be cases with no history provided. Investigators need to be careful with these histories as it is common in natural deaths to not have a history other than finding the child unresponsive. Investigators should take the history, scene, statements, observations, and any known medical information at that time into account before making any judgments. Particular attention should be paid to histories involving feeding, or more importantly, a lack of feeding. A developmental rule of thumb that holds true is that babies like to eat. So what does it mean when a caregiver says that a baby would not take a bottle, or tried and could not take a bottle? It could indicate that the child was already injured at that point in time. Consider that sucking is a reflex, which can be easily triggered with a rub to the cheek. Thus, if an infant can not perform a reflexive action, it may not be able to due to neurological damage already sustained. Documenting the feeding history can be beneficial in establishing timelines and isolating caregivers. Investigators must examine statements for admissions or minimizing actions. "I bounced her on my knee", "I only rubbed her back to wake her" are good examples of trigger words and phrases. Most caregivers will provide these triggers in his or her language.

Identify inconsistencies

So much happens so fast when a case involves a child. From the time the 911 call is received and through the autopsy, information is being gathered and shared through many different individuals. It is critical to document any inconsistencies across histories and interviews, from the EMS responders, hospital personnel, law enforcement and medical examiners or coroners. Investigators must remember that nothing is unimportant!

Do Not Rush!

It is a common inclination to want to go after the person responsible for hurting a child. Rushing the investigative process on an AHT case can result in negative ramifications for the case. First and foremost, try to get preliminary autopsy results *before* beginning the interview/interrogation stage. *Do* get initial statements and interviews, and if a confession is offered, of course take it. The mistake that must be avoided is accepting what is offered initially prior to knowing the extent of the injuries. For example, a confession is obtained and charges are filed against a caregiver the night of the incident. He confesses to shaking and slamming the child's neck against a crib rail. The rail left a clear impression so he could not avoid that detail. However, the autopsy the next morning reveals three skull fractures. Now we have injuries with no explanation. If a caregiver confesses to shaking, is it reasonable to conclude that following the shake, he or she lightly placed the child down on the bed? Not likely, right? Investigators must walk suspects through the *entire* episode, to after he or she place the child down. The preliminary autopsy results can be used to confirm incriminating statements and be used against them in the interrogation. The main rule for investigators in AHT cases is to leave the word "shaking" out of his or her vocabulary. Anyone interacting with the caregivers following the death should adhere to this rule. It may not be known exactly what occurred, and the caregiver should always provide the account to the investigator, not the other way around.

Timeline

In most cases of AHT, the signs and symptoms of injury will occur immediately, with a small percentage presenting with injuries more difficult to age. Timelines play a critical role benefiting both the pathologist and law enforcement as long as each is providing the other with information. Investigators should document all of the activities of the child and caregivers in the hours and potentially days prior to the incident, noting feedings and sleep periods. Perpetrators will often narrow the timeline for investigators by indicating how "fine" the child was, adamantly describing how well the child was after the other caregiver left for work, often implicating himself or herself by indicating he or she was alone with the child at the time of the incident.

Triggers

Most triggers leading to abuse involve unreasonable expectations of children. The number one trigger for AHT is a crying baby. The risk of harm rises when babies have conditions such as reflux and colic. The emergence of language leads to the common trigger of disobedience, as the first word typically learned and repeated is "no". Well, what have children heard from caregivers for the first eighteen months of their lives? It is simple regurgitation of what caregivers say. Those parents who have had a child swear in front of guests understand this concept well! There is the unreasonable expectation that children will do what they are told all the time, so when they refuse situations can escalate. Any references to disobedient behavior could be a red flag. Toilet training is a very common trigger. It is a natural process; however, caregivers like to rush the process before children are ready. When a child is not developmentally ready to be toilet trained, rushing the behavior leads to a regression in behavior, meaning more accidents. So not only does a caregiver get frustrated with an accident, his or her own actions can cause more accidents, more frustration and more anger. The last trigger typically seen with these cases is focused around feeding. Three big changes occur in fairly quick succession in infancy. First, he or she is switched from formula to solid foods. Formula to mushy baby foods is one thing, but it is when the real thing is introduced that the fun begins. Infants will certainly demonstrate taste preferences with baby foods, but at the time when the actual foods are introduced, most have obtained the pincer grasp, using the forefinger and thumb to grab objects. Thus, whatever the caregiver is trying to get in the child's mouth that does not feel or taste good to him or her gets flicked away, typically in the floor or in the caregiver's face. The child is mad anyway because prior to this change he or she had to switch from a nipple to a hard plastic spoon that is shoved in his or her mouth, and switch from a comfortable lap to a high chair. To add insult to injury, he or she gets *restrained* in the high chair! Thus, feeding times go from a nice bonding time to an all-out war. Tempers escalate leading to grabbing, shaking, and throwing.

Language

Investigators should carefully examine any and all statements made by caregivers. What investigators are looking for are trigger words that could give indications of what occurred. It could be that the tone of the language sounds aggressive as well as the words. When words such as "fussy," "wet herself," "grabbed," "smack," etc, or any other negative language appears in histories or statements that should be a red flag and points to pursue with further questioning.

Notification

While notification can hamper any child death investigation, time is of the essence in cases of abusive head trauma. Notification of the proper authorities is critical to the success of a death investigation. In most cases, EMS will be the first agency responding; however, problems can result when the caregivers choose to transport the child by private vehicle. Bear in mind that AHT cases are closed head injuries. Typically there are no signs of external trauma. Most children arrive at the hospital DOA (Dead on Arrival) or pronounced dead shortly after arrival. Hospitals are not responsible for clinically working deceased individuals, so there will be no scans, radiographs, or other diagnostics in these cases that arrive in that condition. Physicians are then left with a dead infant with no obvious reason for the child to be dead, and an initial history from the caregivers. At that point, if a physician believes the parent and also believes there is no obvious trauma, a notification to law enforcement may not occur. When EMS transports, it is more likely that law enforcement will be involved. However, that can also be hampered if EMS fails to make the notification. Precious information can be lost with any delays in notification, as well as the loss of the scene. The rule of thumb is to notify the proper authorities in the event of any unexpected death of a juvenile. A recommended policy is to establish a Dual Response Protocol with dispatch centers. That protocol should state that for any pediatric 911 call involving an unresponsive child or a child with altered mental status, both EMS and law enforcement are dispatched at the same time.

Scenes

Unfortunately, shaking a child does not necessarily involve disturbing the environment. Slamming a child, throwing a child, or impacting the child's head with an object can also not disturb the environment. Impact sites are invaluable when they are discovered, such as on walls; however, when they hit couches, beds, pieces of furniture, or porcelain fixtures, there is not likely to be any evidence. Unless other injuries are present along with the head trauma, blood evidence is not typically found at these scenes. Trace evidence may be more likely, and fluids could be the most beneficial evidence to find. Evidence of bedwetting or toileting accidents could be suggestive of a trigger. Evidence of vomiting, such as on bedding, clothing, or carpet, could indicate that the child was injured and was crashing. Unfortunately, there may be nothing else to physically capture from a scene. What scenes do provide is a context, a picture of that child's system in which it existed. The living conditions, how the child or children are taken care of, available resources, and individuals with caretaking responsibilities all have high evidentiary value. The younger the decedent, the more likely a "secondary scene" will need to be examined. That secondary scene is the floor, where most infants spend the majority of their time. Get in the floor and see what they see from that perspective.

Abdominal Trauma

Abdominal trauma involves impacts or blows to the abdominal area resulting in various injuries to major organs. Typically the injuries occur to the stomach, liver, mesentery, spleen and pancreas. Organs are lacerated, ruptured, torn, and bruised. These injuries can result from punching, stomping, slamming, or striking the area with an object or instrument. Clinically, these children can present with nausea and/or vomiting, lethargy, and unresponsiveness. There may be bruising and/or patterned marks around the abdominal area or back.

Take into account the following investigative considerations:

Histories

As with AHT, the clinical presentation and injuries will not match the history. Common household falls and accidents are typical stories provided by caregivers. Investigators should document any and all inconsistencies across histories and statements.

Timelines

Timelines are critical in abdominal trauma cases due to timing of the injury. Complications in these cases can arise from delays, either in signs and symptoms occurring or death. It can depend on how severely the child was injured. What is observed and when by caregivers will be a focus of the investigation. These delays can range from hours to a day or two, so timelines may need to be extended to capture all persons and settings the child encountered. These children will likely be in pain at some point so it will be important to document *any* changes in behavior noticed by anyone in contact with the child in the day or days prior to the death.

Complications

Delays in symptoms may prove problematic, but other delays can also hinder an investigation. Delays in seeking medical attention can make it more difficult to accurately time an injury. Another consideration is what occurs at the hospital when the children are being treated. It is crucial that law enforcement be notified when an injury is diagnosed or suspected to be non-accidental. As these children are often placed on life support, make sure that notifications are occurring at the time the diagnosis is made or suspected, *not* when the child expires. That mistake can only delay and compromise an investigation further.

Scenes

Initially the scene may appear negative. If the injuries were a result of a beating with hands and feet, there may be no disturbance to the environment. If an object was used, then anything that is not bolted down could be a potential weapon. It will be important to have good documentation of the injuries, including measurements, to compare to the environment. There may be no other physical evidence present other than vomit as most of the injuries in these cases are internal depending on the severity of the beating.

Child Abuse and Neglect

What will be described here as child abuse will be causes of death related to beatings, and other types of abusive injuries. However, other types of homicides discussed in this chapter can be classified as abusive and result in charges of abuse in addition to murder. Neglect can co-occur with abuse or be the sole cause of death in a child. Definitions of both abuse and neglect vary, but share a common denominator: intention. Abusive deaths involve beatings resulting in bruising and fractures, as well as burns. Healing injuries from prior assaults may also be present in these cases.

Bruising

The rule regarding bruising is that they can not be accurately aged by examining the color of the bruise. Simply stated, an individual can not look at a bruise and say how old it may be. Everyone bruises differently so red may not always mean *new* or *fresh*. From a pathological perspective, the doctors can scientifically test the tissue and provide an age for the hemorrhage. From an investigative perspective, there are three key factors about bruising to take into consideration: size, shape and location. When examining a non-mobile infant, one that is not yet pulling up, crawling or walking, there should be no bruises, period. Children bruise by interacting with their environment, thus if they can not move around in that environment there should be no bruises. Pay attention to histories provided by caregivers in cases of marks or bruises on infants. When examining a mobile child, it is common to find bruises. That would indicate they are *active children*! Now take into account the three key factors about bruising.

What does the size of the bruise suggest?

The child came into contact with a significant object or surface to create the bruise. Whatever history is provided to explain the mark should match the mark. The "I don't know how that bruise got there" story typically will not suffice when an atypically sized bruise is observed. Whenever possible, investigators should get a reconstruction of what occurred.

What does the shape of the bruise suggest?

The mere fact that there is a pattern to a bruise should be a red flag, to be taken into consideration with the provided explanation. Any time a child is struck with an object, it has the potential to leave an imprint. The pressure of the object pushes the blood to the edges, leaving blanching in the middle with a red outline. Sometimes the edges can be abraded if the object has edges. For example, a broomstick handle may only leave an imprint whereas a piece of molding may cause abrasions on the edges. The bottom line is there will be a mark or bruise that can be measured. If there is a patterned mark of any kind investigators must measure it, photograph it, and search the environment for any object matching those dimensions. Photographs should be taken as soon as possible as the bruises may fade quickly, which can mean loss of shape and dimension. Investigators should not let his or her imagination limit the search for potential weapons. Children are beaten with weapons of opportunity, whatever is within reach at the time. If an object is not bolted to the floor, it has the potential to be used. Weapons do not walk away from the scene, they will still be there as they are typically part of the everyday environment. Investigators should provide the pathologist with possible objects obtained during the investigation so he or she can provide an opinion as to whether the object is consistent or inconsistent with the injuries.

What does the location of the bruise suggest?

As children are typically moving forward, the frontal plane takes the brunt of the everyday activities. The bony prominences such as the face, chin, elbows, and knees get bruised easily. Thus typical bruising in these areas is somewhat expected, given the age and activities of the child. Excessive bruising or bruising of the softer areas, such as the abdominal area should be questioned. Now consider the backside, and how a bruise would occur accidentally on the back. Yes, it is possible to fall backwards and get a bruise. However, children are not likely to exhibit patterned marks or excessive bruising in areas they can not reach. Red flags should be raised with marks and bruising on the upper and lower back, buttocks or legs. Beware of Mongolian Spots on children which typically occur in these areas. A Mongolian Spot can be distinguished from a bruise in that they are typically the same color throughout the mark. At autopsy, the pathologist can cut across the mark and examine the underlying tissue for hemorrhage. There will be no hemorrhage under a Mongolian Spot. Mongolian Spots are more common in darker skinned races and ethnicities, and there should be documentation of the marks in the birth records or pediatric records.

Fractures

Common sites of fractures in abuse cases involve the ribs, long bones of the arms and legs, and skull. Rib and skull fractures commonly co-occur with abusive head trauma. Metaphyseal fractures, or bucket handle fractures, can occur at the joints where growth plates have not fused together in children. These types of fractures are strongly indicative of abuse. Bones are strong and designed to take force, just not certain types of force. So torsion or twisting forces and direct impacts result in breaks. It will be important to have a skeletal survey done on children, either at the autopsy or as part of the clinical work-up if the child goes to the hospital. Investigative considerations will include the following:

Timing

Acute fractures are those occurring at the time of death. If fractures are present and healing, then they have most likely been present a minimum of 7–10 days. A pediatric radiologist is the best resource for these cases. They will be able to accurately date the fractures. It will be important to establish a firm timeline to document the history of abuse when applicable.

History

Histories associated with fractures will often involve falls or household accidents. Accidents can result in fractures so it will be critical to weigh the provided history carefully. The pathologist will be able to assist in ruling out potential accidental causes. If old and healing fractures are present, then the child most likely experienced considerable pain at the onset of the injury. Anyone having contact with the child during that time should be interviewed. Investigators should pay particular attention to observations that the child was acting atypical. Infants with rib fractures may *not* want to be picked up or squeezed or may be fussy. Children with untreated broken legs or arms may not be able to use those limbs normally, or have limited range of motion or a visible deformity. Untreated spiral fractures can actually result in the shortening of a limb, such as a half-inch difference in the legs of a two-year-old that suffered from an untreated femur fracture. That should result in a noticeable limp. Any history that suggests that the child was fine, and played and acted normally would be a suspicious history.

Statements

From spontaneous statements made at the scene to formal written statements, examine the words for clues into how a fracture may have occurred. Words such as "fell," "tripped," "drop," "grab," or "squeezed," could be associated with fractures. Words such as these may give the investigator a hint that can be exploited. Particularly with skull fractures, it is always interesting to see what caregivers say initially and how that progresses toward a more accurate portrayal. With multiple skull fractures the investigator should let the suspect provide the number of impacts first. Investigators must never play his or her hand. Caregivers will have to get the number right and the location right, otherwise he or she is lying. A suspect in a blunt force trauma case consistently provided three impacts in his histories, matching the three skull fractures found at autopsy. Unfortunately for him, in subsequent statements he could never get the location of the fractures correct.

Burns

Burns are, without question, the most despicable type of injury that can be inflicted upon a child. With other types of trauma, perpetrators may not necessarily see the injuries he or she has caused, or grasp the extent of the damage caused by his or her actions. However, it is impossible to *not* know the suffering and pain caused by a burn. It can be seen, heard, and potentially smelled by the perpetrator. The target age range for burns is typically one to five years. The triggers associated with burns are similar to those found in abusive head trauma cases. Investigators should take into account the following considerations when investigating a burn case:

- Patterned burns—Any item in the child's environment that can be heated could be a potential cause of a burn. The wound must be carefully examined and the pattern compared to items in the environment.
- Lines of demarcation—This will actually be a line dividing an area of the body that is burned from an area that is not burned. For example, if they submerse the arm to just above the elbow, there will be a line delineating the two areas.
- Symmetry—Inflicted burns appear uniform, symmetrical and organized. Accidental burns appear random and disorganized. Accidental burns occasionally have directional flow patterns or spatter patterns, as when a pot spills off of the stove.

Neglect can take many forms. However, neglect resulting in death takes it to the extreme. It will typically manifest in one of two ways, physical neglect and lack of supervision.

Physical neglect results in the child dying from complications of malnutrition and lack of appropriate care. Frankly, if an investigator has ever experienced a case such as this, it is never forgotten. The physical evidence will speak for itself. Medical neglect can result in physical illness, permanent disability, or death.

The other form of neglect involves lack of supervision, resulting in the death of the child. For example, a three-year-old child wandering away from home while the babysitter sleeps off last night's drunk on the couch. The child could end up in the highway, in the neighbor's pool, or in the backyard with the chained dog. Cases like these rise to the level of criminal negligence, with accompanying charges.

Munchausen Syndrome By Proxy

A quick Internet search for Munchausen Syndrome By Proxy, or MSBP, will yield a few hundred thousand potential websites related to the topic. A maze of definitions, terminology, symptoms, and diagnostics are associated with the disorder. We will examine the fundamentals of MSBP from the investigative perspective. First and foremost, it is abuse. In cases where the abuse leads to the death of the child, it is a homicide. Whether referred to as a disorder, condition, or sickness does not change the fact that it is the intentional act of a caregiver against a child. Two forms are generally recognized, with caregivers falsifying symptoms and conditions, or more commonly creating illness and symptoms through abusive tactics. Physical abuse, injections of toxic materials, food poisoning, these are just the tip of the iceberg of the potential methods used by caregivers to make a child sick. As the medical treatments escalate in an effort to identify and cure the "illness", unsuspecting physicians then become a tool for abusive caregivers.

The most common perpetrator in these cases will be mothers, although fathers have also been identified. Typical characteristics include the following:

- Intrinsically rewarded behavior — It is attention-seeking behavior so do not focus on external motivations. It is definitely not about the money, as many will incur exorbitant medical bills.
- No medical explanation or cause can be identified — This makes sense given that the symptoms are being created! However, the illnesses and symptoms created can mimic real conditions and make it difficult for medical providers to differentiate true illness from falsified conditions.
- Persistent symptoms and ineffective treatments — These caregivers develop a compulsion to offend, thus the symptoms are not alleviated by treatments. Even when put in video monitored rooms, caregivers will offend against the child.
- Symptoms miraculously disappear when child is separated from the offending caregiver — This should confirm the suspicions of the treating physician, and provide the proof necessary for criminal charges and actions by child protection services to proceed.
- Involvement and attention — Typically the caregiver's attention is not always focused on the child, and his or her in-

volvement is more with medical personnel. Different professionals will perceive this aspect through varying lenses. As a child development specialist, my perception focuses on the dynamic between caregiver and child. That dynamic in these cases will be off. The child becomes a tool to the caregiver and that will become apparent in his or her interactions with the child.

- More, more, more!—When suggestions for a different medication, or new treatment, or surgical procedure are made by a medical professional, the caregiver will likely jump at the chance. The "more, more, more" effect means he or she will try anything regardless of the cost to the child. When the child becomes a tool to the parent, it affects the parent/child dynamic which should be observed.
- Doctor shopping—Have child, will travel. Caregivers will move around to different doctors to stay under the radar of physicians, but also to pursue new and specialized doctors and treatments. He or she may have to seek physicians outside of his or her local area if he or she has been "flagged" by local providers. The caregiver may travel into neighboring counties or states, so investigators should be prepared to extend the boundaries when looking for medical records.

The perpetrators in these cases are often identified by a medical professional. As symptoms can mimic real illnesses, it may not be immediately apparent that anything suspicious is occurring. But once the medical professional acknowledges his or her suspicions, a team approach is launched. There will typically be a team within hospitals that handles these types of cases. In addition, child protection services, mental health, prosecutors, and law enforcement will comprise the investigative team. While a physician may have suspicions, proving those suspicions can be a delicate matter. These cases require complete communication and cooperation between all professionals involved. The proverbial brick wall may get hit when the abuse can not be proven. Law enforcement and child protection services will not be able to pursue actions without that proof. It is important for all involved to continue to work together on obtaining the necessary proof against the caregiver. Many hospitals have video monitored rooms to try to capture abusive episodes on tape.

Investigative considerations will include the following:

Playing dumb

These caregivers are not to be taken lightly. He or she is smart and manipulative. The caregivers do have a tendency to believe that the professionals are not smart enough to catch on to his or her actions. Sometimes validating his or her beliefs creates a false sense of security, and causes him or her to make mistakes.

Proof

Ideally, the autopsy will provide a cause for the child's death. Additional proof of what was being done to the child may be provided in the medical history and agency history.

Patterns

Fortunately, these caregivers get regimented in his or her abuse. Depending on the tactic, it may occur on a particular day, or during a specific time period during the day. For example, injections may have to occur during times when other caregivers are not at home, or poisonings occur at meal times. Investigators should examine the day to day activities for patterns in behavior, or changes in routines. Another pattern to examine is the progression of illnesses and symptoms. A thorough investigation into MSBP deaths will require extensive examination of medical records. The pattern to watch for is a subtle change in the type of illness or symptom. Essentially it will be a change in tactic reflected by a change in the child's exhibited symptoms or reported illness. The caregiver may have to alter tactics if the child ages out of one tactic, or the desired effect is not occurring anymore. For example, suppose the caregiver started with intentional suffocation on an infant. The medical history may reflect respiratory symptoms or possible seizure disorder. However, infants grow into young children who can verbalize. Thus, they must switch gears. Respiratory illnesses and other symptoms may shift towards more neurological symptoms, intestinal disorders, etc. These patterns are not a given, meaning that whether or not the patterns are present depends on many factors. These factors can include what the caregiver chooses to do to the child, if they have to switch tactics, and age of the child when the caregiver started, to name a few.

These cases are similar to assembling a five hundred piece puzzle. MSBP cases are complicated, require immense amounts of time and effort, and are successfully completed through attention to detail and interdisciplinary collaboration.

Guns

Gun homicides in children are typically more common in the older age ranges. Many involve criminal activity such as drugs or gangs, and are juvenile to juvenile shootings. Gun deaths in children in the younger age ranges, typically under ten years of age, are less common and are sometimes related to domestic violence. For example, an estranged spouse returns to shoot the mother and child. Murder-suicides may occur in those situations. Gun cases involving children are typically approached in the same manner as adult shootings, with the exception of building a comprehensive history on the shooter and family in domestic or familial shootings. Investigators should make sure the following areas are addressed in gun related homicides:

- Gun—Whose weapon was it? This is most important in cases of young perpetrators. Good luck getting any reliable information on weapons used in drug or gang related shootings!
- History—Investigators should check law enforcement, social service, and domestic violence history on the shooter and family, in applicable cases.
- Social history—Investigators need to examine the system for any issues going on with the family that could have precipitated the death.

Drowning

Drowning homicides are most likely to occur in younger children and infants, given their size and ability of an adult to physically overpower them. Drowning deaths are generally nonspecific pathologically, so there may be no findings to definitively confirm drowning. Thus the investigation becomes even more critical. External bruising or marks may be present to suggest a struggle. The scene, history, and statements will hopefully provide an indication of the actual circumstances. Cases vary, but common histories include children being "found in the tub" and removed, discovered unresponsive but wet, or clothed but the scene is suspiciously damp. Investigators should examine statements for any indicators or trigger words to suggest something occurred to frustrate or anger the caregiver. With a potential negative autopsy, the scene investigation and statements may be the pieces that determine the manner.

Poisoning

Many substances are toxic to children, so poisoning cases can pose unique challenges. The primary challenge may be identifying the toxin. In the ideal case, the child exhibits signs of illness prior to dying. As that may not be a given in every case, the scene details and history become the critical pieces of the investigation.

- What does the scene suggest — Investigators should look for any possible toxins, which could include prescription medications, OTC, cleaners, or pesticides and look for any signs that the child was sick or vomited anywhere in the residence.
- What does the history suggest — Is the history offered vague or does the caregiver suggest the child "ate" something or "got into" something? It is possible to only get the standard, "threw up and went limp" history with these cases.

- What do other agencies and professionals suggest—Investigators should examine medical records and child protection services records for any indicators of previous incidences.

Investigators must bear in mind that when initially in the scene, it may not be known that a toxin is involved. It could be later, from additional investigation or toxicology results, that it is suspected. Thus, it is feasible that an investigator would be looking for specific toxins upon returning to the scene. The more details that can be gathered related to the possible toxin, the more specific the tests can be. For example, base screens for alcohol and drugs may not reveal other chemicals and vice versa. Remember that pathologists and toxicologists will not always know what to test for unless provided specific details.

Fire

Fortunately, it is uncommon for homicides of children to occur by fire. As all fires, especially those involving fatalities, are investigated by more than one agency (i.e., law enforcement, fire marshal, insurance investigators) these cases rarely slip through the cracks. Perpetrators may kill the child by other means and then set the house of fire. Depending on the extent of the thermal injuries, the pathologist can determine the exact cause of death and whether or not the child was deceased at the time of the fire. For example, a father shoots his daughter and torches the house. Despite the charring of the remains, the bullet wound is discernible at the autopsy, so the cause is not actually the fire. Ssshh, do not tell perspective perpetrators that fire does not actually destroy all evidence! Unfortunately, fire cases are not always that cut and dried. When a death occurs in a fire, and it is determined the child died from the fire specifically, either from the thermal injuries or carbon monoxide poisoning, it must then be determined that the fire was intentionally set. It may be important to rule out that the perpetrator did something to incapacitate the child so he or she did not escape the fire. For example, giving the child medication to sleep or disarm fire alarms. The scenes may provide a picture of this as well, if the child was found in the bed, or in a position indicating they were looking for a way out or a hiding place.

Other Homicides

There are countless ways for perpetrators to take out frustrations on a child, and juveniles to offend other juveniles. Fights, stabbings, and beatings often result in youth on youth related deaths. Other types of homicides can include motor vehicles, alcohol toxicity, torture and rape, and abductions. True predators are an entirely different animal.

Summary

If there is a silver lining to these cases it is this, typically the perpetrator is right in front of the investigator. Mothers, fathers, and boyfriends top the list of perpetrators with other relatives to follow. It is uncommon for the perpetrator to *not* be related or otherwise known in some way to the child. The recipe for success with homicides of children is a full cup of details, two cups of knowledge and expertise, one can of timeline, prepared in a bowl of collaboration and mix in pinch of patience. The most difficult thing a detective will ever do is sit across a table during an interview or interrogation and be nice to someone he or she suspects just murdered a child. Investigators will always catch more flies with honey. They must always remember to keep their emotions in check.

Case Examples

The following examples provide a brief initial history, similar to what is relayed to medical examiners, coroners and pathologist upon initial report. Take each history and design an inquiry, develop questions for the pathologist and all potentially involved agencies, and list possible causes of death. Readers can check their inquiries against the full analysis provided in Appendix A.

1) EMS responded to call for an unresponsive 9 month old. Visible bruising, mother's boyfriend reported child fell from crib. Law enforcement notified and responded to the scene. Child pronounced at the hospital.

2) 16-year-old female presented to ER with abdominal pains and bleeding. Examination showed recent birth. Authorities were notified and contacted family. A search was conducted at the home and a deceased newborn was discovered in the trash.

3) 2-year-old presented to ER. History of vomiting, no external trauma, some bruising noted on forehead and child was wet.

Investigation to Do List

❑ Document initial history and circumstances
❑ Secure statements of individuals with the child at the time
❑ Establish who had supervising or had physical custody of the child at the time
❑ Document positions and locations
❑ Document time LSA
❑ Document all resuscitation attempts
❑ Obtain reconstructions
❑ Obtain relevant medical histories
❑ Document any prior deaths and where occurred
❑ Identify triggers and red flags within histories and statements
❑ Document any external marks or indicators of trauma
❑ Establish any past or current histories with local agencies
❑ Make sure all scenes are secured and appropriately processed
❑ Document scenes (photographs, diagrams, descriptions)
❑ Provide pathologists with scene information as needed or requested
❑ Obtain preliminary autopsy results

❑   Obtain emergency room records when applicable
❑   Obtain statements and histories for any healing injuries when
     applicable
❑   Document involved agency contacts and maintain communication
❑   Document timelines appropriate to the circumstances

CHAPTER 8

UNDETERMINED

Parents should come with instructions.

—Shanna, age 14

A six-year-old female is found deceased at home. Parents awoke to find child not breathing in the bed. No anatomic cause of death found.

Pathologists have four other choices for manner of death before ruling a death as undetermined. The ruling of undetermined as a manner of death can be frustrating to investigators. To begin, we need to clarify what undetermined can mean in a death case. Undetermined manner of death means that the *how* can not be accurately determined in a fatality. For example, if a youth is found with a gunshot wound to the head, the cause of death is the gunshot wound to the head. However, conflicting investigative details from family, friends, and/or witnesses make it impossible to determine if the wound was self-inflicted or accidental. Now, the opposite can also be true, where the manner is known due to the circumstances, but the *cause* of death is undetermined. It is feasible to have a homicide or other manner of death, with no exact cause of death.

Why is it important to make these distinctions with the term undetermined? When the ruling of undetermined is uttered, there is a tendency for investigations to come to a screeching halt. The brick wall has been hit, so to speak, and it seems there is no where else to go with the investigation. Cases are ruled undetermined for two reasons, either too much information or not enough. Too much information could indicate that there are conflicting details rendering it impossible to determine the exact circumstances. The body can also provide too much information, meaning that there could be findings to suggest more than one way the child could have died. The body can also provide little information and no concrete answers. There could be a multitude of findings at the autopsy, but none that resulted in or relate to the death. When an investigation is not conducted, regardless of the reason, the pathologist likely has no circumstances or scene to combine with the autopsy results. That lack of information can easily lead to a ruling of undetermined. There will also be the cases where there is no way to rule in or rule out a specific manner. Remember this rule: cause and manner can always be changed.

If more information comes to light, whether a month after or five years after the death, the original paperwork can be amended to reflect the accurate cause and manner of death. In essence, an undetermined case can always remain open pending further information.

There will undoubtedly be cases where little is known at the onset, and it is not likely any additional information will ever be known. What is important is that the cases are given every consideration and effort to ensure that the details are gathered to the fullest extent possible. It could be that one person has one detail that could sway the determination in another direction. Medicolegal investigations will continue as long as necessary in an attempt to reach a final conclusion. A ruling of undetermined should never prohibit an agency from conducting a thorough investigation, to the extent possible.

Summary

The ruling of undetermined manner of death indicates that one of the other four options is not appropriate, or can not be definitively proven. In some cases it can be difficult for the families to accept. It provides no tangible reason or explanation. For investigators, it often means the end of a case. It can not be emphasized strongly enough that any additional information that is obtained should be shared with pathologists in the event it could change the manner. There is no checklist provided for this chapter. A thorough investigation will have included all of the details provided in previous chapters. Arriving at the ruling of undetermined means investigative inquiries *at that point* have been exhausted.

Case Examples

The following examples provide a brief initial history, similar to what is relayed to medical examiners, coroners and pathologist upon initial report. Take each history and design an inquiry, develop questions for the pathologist and all potentially involved agencies, and list possible causes of death. Readers can check their inquiries against the full analysis provided in Appendix A.

1) 4 month old found dead in bed with mother and sibling.
2) 13 month old found deceased in crib.
3) 18 month old reportedly lethargic at home.

CHAPTER 9

Interviewing Families

The child supplies the power but the parents have to do the steering.

—Benjamin Spock

While talking to people is a skill possessed by most in law enforcement, communicating with and gathering information from families after the loss of a child takes those skills to an entirely different level. It requires sensitivity, respect, and the ability to set aside the role of "detective" and interact as another parent or just simply as another person. As with most skills, there will be some professionals better suited to dealing with families than others. Everyone has their own comfort zone that best works for them in these situations, and it is just a matter of finding that individual style that families respond to. We will address the principles and techniques necessary for gathering the most information from families while building a relationship with them which results in more successful investigations.

Introductions

When and where an investigator first meets families will likely vary from case to case. In most instances it will be either the original scene or hospital. Either way it will be an emotionally charged and chaotic environment. There has been a death, so it is what it is, and it is up to the investigator to make it work to their benefit. It will be important to establish who it is you are interviewing and their relationship to the child. I may speak differently to a biological parent than another relative or adult caretaker. I learned years ago to not make assumptions about who may be the parent!

It is likely that no one knows anything except that the child is deceased at this point. So we have to gather every piece of information possible during a very difficult time from the very people who are suffering the most. The formal interviews will come later, right now this is about establishing rapport and gaining the family's trust and getting everything from them possible. There is no ideal time.

Everyone is a victim in these cases. They have suffered a loss. The hows and whys will rise to the surface later. But if a parent or caregiver is treated like a suspect at the onset, particularly when they know they did nothing to their child, the information flow will come to a grinding halt and so goes the investigation. Treat them appropriately if/when they become a suspect, however families are not going to tolerate anything remotely suggestive or accusatory, nor should they when they did nothing to cause the death of their child. The numbers do not lie, and the majority of deaths in children are accidental or natural. Even if it turns into a homicide investigation, being nice to your suspect goes much further in these cases as a general rule if you do not want them to ask for a lawyer.

Families will be curious as to why law enforcement is even present. I suggest framing it somehow under "standard procedure" so that they do not feel singled out. It is a good idea to let them know there will be some questions that will need to be answered and any information obtained will be used to figure out exactly what happened to their child. They want answers more than you do so if you become the route by which they get those answers, you should have their full cooperation. However, they have just had the proverbial rug yanked out from underneath them. Their heads are spinning, everyone is asking them questions, and no one can give *them* any answers. So you may find yourself repeating why you are there, what information you need, and how that information will be used.

Core Principles

Emotion—This refers to the emotions of the investigator. Any one of these cases has the potential to be personal to professionals. Perhaps you are a parent of a child the same age, or are just back to work from maternity leave and now have to investigate the death of a baby. Investigators must maintain their objectivity. I am certainly not suggesting everyone be stoic and stone-faced, but it will hinder efforts to gather information if you and the parent both fall apart. While there is no shame in crying, if a case is too personal for an investigator, the case should be handled by someone else.

Language—There are three aspects of language that investigators need to understand during the course of an investigation. The first is the tense used in reference to the child. Whatever tense the parent uses is what the investigator should use. They will make the cognitive shift from present to past on their own, so just mirror their words. The second aspect is the use of the word "crime." For law enforcement purposes it is just part of the everyday vernacular. Specific times to avoid using it would be when referring to the scene itself. Now if your agency vehicles have Crime Scene Unit plastered all over the side, it will be difficult to avoid the issue when it is parked in the driveway outside the scene. However, make every attempt to just use the word 'scene' alone, because as soon as the word crime creeps in, they are likely to interpret that as being accused. Also, when making introductions try to just use first names and not titles. So let's say the detective and the crime scene photographer are going into the home. I would suggest introducing them as "Ron," not " 'Ron from the crime scene unit." Again, if it is plastered all over everyone's jackets in the house, you may not be able to avoid answering questions. The third aspect to definitely take into consideration is the child's name itself. Do not assume that you as the investigator can sit down and start talking to a parent about their child 'John'. It is respectful and sensitive to ask the child's name, or what he/she was called and ask if you may call him/her by that name. If you say 'John' and his name was Jonathon, you just disrespected their child. It is a small effort that takes only seconds to accomplish but the payoff is well worth it. They want to know you are vested in their child's case, because if they sense you are not then why should *they* bother engaging with *you*?

Nonverbal—Do not overanalyze someone's nonverbal behaviors when they are experiencing grief. They are grieving! The grief response in these particular cases is very intense and riddled with guilt over things they had no control over. That can not be interpreted as anything but parental response in the loss of a child, in most cases. True guilty behaviors will rise to the surface all on their own. The crucial point here is that investigators not fall prey to the ridiculous notion of "emotionally appropriate" behavior. There is no such thing, especially under these conditions. Investigators should also be aware of their own nonverbal behaviors and not project them onto parents or caregivers. Their sensitivity levels will be extremely high and the slightest miscue, whether intentional or not, just may push them over the edge.

Obstacles

Emotion—While the investigator's emotion is a principle that guides the process, the parent or caregiver's emotion is an obstacle that must be handled respectfully and sensitively. Their emotions are like a roller coaster with high peaks and low deep dips. When their emotions are spiking (topping the peaks) it will be more difficult to get them to focus; however, when they come down off the peak (and they will!) they will be much more amenable to interviewing. The truth is that crying adults make other adults very nervous, which creates a hesitancy to speak with parents when they are upset. There will not be an "easy" time, and waiting creates a risk of losing information. Timing your approach and questions during those 'dips' and they will cooperate fully. Remember, they want answers more than you do!

Joint Interviews—Joint interviews are not typically recommended for several reasons. First, parents and caregivers are likely to be overwhelmed with too many people, especially if more than one person is asking questions. Second, continuity should be maintained whenever possible. It will require full cooperation across agencies and professionals can decide amongst themselves who should do the interview, but in death investigations the lead interviewer should be the person who will be involved for the duration of the investigation. That role is typically held by law enforcement.

Previous Interviews—It is critical that investigators find out at the onset of an investigation how many other people may have talked with families, what was said, and what they may or may not already know. In most instances of child deaths, investigations originate at the hospital. So it is possible that nurses, doctors, clergy, hospital social workers or others may have questioned families before law enforcement even arrives.

Investigators will want to know the details of any previous communications with families to better prepare for their own interviews.

Techniques

Free Association—Good news! Getting parents and caregivers to talk about their child is actually very easy. They enjoy telling anyone else about their child and what makes them so special. The relationship, whether it is positive or negative, between the person being interviewed and the child will become evident through their language, facial expressions, and overall tone of the conversation. It is best to start at a general point and work towards the time of the death. For example, if the decedent is an infant the investigator can begin with the pregnancy or birth and ask questions that lead them gradually towards the day of the death. In older children, it may work better to start with what kind of person the child was, what activities did they enjoy, what was their personality like, and then ease in to the time surrounding the death. The more they talk, the clearer the picture of the relationship becomes.

Show Me—The "show me" principle is simply about respecting the family's turf. Consider the environment in which the child lived sacred territory and be sensitive and respectful of the fact that the family does not want their reminders of the child disturbed. This is not difficult nor will it interfere in the processing of the scene. It simply means when the investigator goes into the family's home, ask them to "show me where your child was sleeping/playing/laying" instead of "if you'll stay in the living room and tell me where your child's room is." Success lies in how families are treated, and respect and sensitivity will result in greater rewards. In homicides, this principle may or may not be adhered to, depending on what is known when. If investigators are just meeting the family and the autopsy has not even occurred, then nothing is known. Refer back to the introductions section of this chapter for a refresher.

Preplanning Questions—Timing is a tremendous disadvantage in child death cases. Investigators like to be prepared and have a plan for their questions, which is unfortunately hard to do in these circumstances. The lack of known medical information at the onset of child deaths is the main problem with attempting to pre-plan questions. In most cases, children are transported to hospitals from the original scenes and pronounced DOA or shortly thereafter. When that happens, no diagnostics are performed. For investigators, that means that hospital personnel can not tell them anything reliable about how the child died. Without diagnostics, the only opinion that can be given with 100% medical certainty is that the child is deceased. So the next logical place to get information is the autopsy. Unfortunately, depending on when the child dies, the autopsy may not take place until the next day. Without known and reliable medical information, it is recommended that investigators wait on preliminary autopsy results before planning for formal interviews or interrogations. In the meantime, gather as many pertinent details surrounding the circumstances of the death as possible.

Summary

The best investigative tool that any investigator can have when handling child death cases is patience. Unless someone has suffered this kind of loss themselves, we can never know what these families experience. We must bear in mind that all semblance of control of their lives has been tragically yanked from their hands. They are either being crowded with comfort from all directions, or bombarded with questions they are not able to answer. Being patient, giving them a direction to pursue (finding out what happened to their child), can return a small amount of control to their lives. Patience and respect demonstrate to families that you are in fact vested in their child, which results in much more cooperation and successful investigations.

CHAPTER 10

Reconstructions

It's so much darker when a light goes out than it would have been if it had never shone."
— John Steinbeck, The Winter of Our Discontent

For the past several years, there has been a national effort to obtain better information in infant death investigations by conducting reconstructions. They truly are an investigator's best tool in these types of cases, and they can be used in other types of deaths as well. A reconstruction with caregivers serves several key purposes. First, it helps pathologists reach the most accurate and appropriate cause and manner of death. Second, it can maximize the amount of information gathered and provide the proper context to the death. Lastly, reconstructions can be used to both confirm and refute histories. This chapter will detail the specific steps necessary for conducting a reconstruction in deaths of infants under one year of age.

Equipment

Doll—The doll can be the most important or least important part of the process. Yes, it can be used to demonstrate positions, but the same thing can be accomplished with a stuffed animal because the caregiver simply can not handle a baby doll yet. Do not spend a lot of money on a doll. Dolls with moveable parts are preferable but avoid dolls with detachable parts. They will fall off at the wrong time! Good ones can be picked up at toy stores and thrift stores for anywhere from $10–$50 so do shop around. Some recommend having several dolls of varying ethnicities so that professionals can be culturally sensitive with the process. The important point to remember is that the process is guided by the caregivers and we use what makes them comfortable. It is not a matter of what doll they prefer, but whether they are comfortable with a doll at all. If not, use a pillow, stuffed animal, whatever gets the job done and keeps them engaged in the process. If the doll is too much for them to handle, then get creative! The dolls are not named and should be handled respectfully in front of caregivers.

Bag—The bag is a must. Never walk into a home to do a reconstruction with a doll in your arms. The bag should have some type of closure so the doll is completely out of sight until it is time to begin the reconstruction. Keeping the bag closed also ensures that siblings that may be in the home do not get into your things. I try to leave the bag by the door so while I am meeting and talking with the family, it is not a focal point. Receiving blankets and other accessories can be kept in the bag and incorporated into the reconstructions as needed.

Camera/Video—Either still shots or video of the reconstruction are appropriate. Different agencies have different preferences and policies. It is recommended that a copy of the pictures or video be provided to the pathologist conducting the autopsy. In a suspicious death, a video of the reconstruction may be more beneficial.

Checklist—Most jurisdictions use some type of checklist or investigation form for child deaths. The SUIDI Form (Sudden Unexplained Infant Death Investigation) is available through the Centers for Disease Control. Other agencies, typically either law enforcement or medical examiner/coroner, have developed their own version of infant/child death investigation checklists. Whatever the version, it allows investigators to collect the specific details necessary to make the best determinations of cause and manner in these deaths. It can serve as a transition into the reconstruction process.

Approach

THE APPROACH IS THE MOST CRITICAL PART OF THE PROCESS. If the approach is not done properly, it is not likely that the caregiver will agree to the reconstruction. Remember that it is voluntary! Once the issue of a reconstruction has been broached, families will probably want to know why they need to participate. This explanation can make or break the process so make sure you are clear with them: The information gathered during the reconstruction process is provided to the medical examiner/coroner/pathologist, and is combined with the other information you have already given us, so that we can figure out exactly what happened to your child. If they believe that this process will help them find out what happened to their child, they will do it. The next step is to go over exactly what the reconstruction entails beforehand, so they know what to expect and can ask questions. The caregivers set the pace and may need to stop now and then during the process so do not set a time limit for the reconstruction or schedule things around it. *They* are helping *you* so give them your undivided attention. Also, cut off all electronic devices attached to your person while doing a reconstruction — no distractions.

Details

The critical details will relate to the immediate sleep environment and positions of the infant. The *position when placed* will be the initial phase of the reconstruction. Investigators will want to ask the caregiver exactly how the child was placed when last seen alive. Typical placements will include on their back, side, stomach, and propped. If they are propped, have them demonstrate how and with what. Commercial wedges may be used or rolled blankets are sometimes used to prop babies to prevent them from rolling. It is sometimes recommended with babies having reflux that a wedge be placed underneath the sleeping surface to give them a slightly angled sleep position. This should be documented accordingly. If infants are placed on their stomachs, it is critical to document the placement of the face/neck, specifically if they were laid down with the face to the left, right or literally face down. The caregivers will need to describe what items were in the immediate sleep environment. Depending on when the reconstruction occurs, items may have been collected during the processing of the scene. Document any blankets, pillows, toys or other items that were around the child at the time. If co-sleeping is part of the history, the caregiver will need to demonstrate exactly how they went to sleep with the child. If they are unable or unwilling, it is fine if another person demonstrates at the direction of the caregiver.

The next phase will be demonstrating the *position when found*. If the same person placed and found the child then it can be one continuous reconstruction. If two different caregivers were involved then there will need to be a separate reconstruction with each individual. As with the first phase of the reconstruction, have the caregiver demonstrate exactly how they found the child. It is important to document face/neck placements, as well as any items around or surrounding the face. Provide descriptions of those items, such as the type of material and thickness. These details help the pathologist determine if there was a possibility of asphyxiation or smothering. At this point in the reconstruction, the caregiver may realize that they might have accidentally asphyxiated their child while sleeping. Be prepared to redirect them and keep them engaged in the process. What they think happened may not necessarily be what happened. The reconstruction is only a piece of the puzzle and it is important to emphasize with the caregivers that the pathologist makes the final determination.

Investigators can clarify specific details as they go through the reconstruction or at the conclusion. Each case will vary so there are no strict rules governing the process, but it will be important to give the caregivers the opportunity to ask questions. It is not recommended that investigators voice any conclusions or give any opinions as to cause and manner at this time.

Exit Strategy

The goal of the exit strategy is to be able to go back to the home and maintain communication with the family through the course of the investigation. So how professionals handle themselves with the family throughout the reconstruction and investigative process is critical. Thus, concluding the reconstruction on a positive note is important. In any circumstance, expressing condolences is appropriate. However, never express understanding, in the form of 'I know this is hard', 'I know how you must be feeling'. Parents and caregivers find this offensive, and it will upset and anger them because you can not possibly know what they are experiencing.

Investigators should make sure that families know what to expect from this point forward in the investigation. A few critical issues to remember to address with families include:

Selecting a funeral home—This is the last thing on their minds. The funeral homes take care of so many details and provide support to the families.

Autopsy—Families will likely ask if they can refuse the autopsy. In most instances that will not be possible. Investigators should inform the families of when results (preliminary and final) might be available, or how long the investigation may take.

Contacts—Families should have contact information for not only the investigators, but also the pathology facility. They should feel comfortable calling either with questions about the autopsy and/or the investigation.

Summary

Investigators should not view the reconstruction process as a negative or tortuous thing to do *to* families, but rather as a step in the investigation done *with* the family. They want answers and understand the reconstruction is a means to that end. When the necessary time and patience is put into the process, the families will be more appreciative than investigators might think. The pathologists will welcome the additional information and the positive effect the reconstruction has on final determinations in these difficult cases.

APPENDIX A

CASE ANALYSES

Remember that the baseline information should be established for every case. It is understood that for some cases and scenes, the baseline information will vary. These analyses represent questions asked that are guided by the baseline information obtained. They demonstrate the direction investigations often take.

Chapter 4: Natural Death Cases

The cases and investigative information presented here do not represent actual cases or persons. Typical scenarios for child deaths have been fictionalized for educational purposes.

Case #1 —

18 month old found deceased in crib at home. Child has history of mental retardation. Scene noted to be filthy with what appears to be vomit in the crib. One other sibling in home.

Inquiry:

1) LSA and activity at that time?
2) Members of household?
3) Age of sibling
4) Recent and past medical history, history relevant to vomiting?
5) Medications?
6) Developmental history?

7) History of abuse or neglect?
8) Family/Social history?

Questions for pathologist:
1) Significance of bruises?
2) Gross findings?
3) Toxicology?

Questions for other agencies:
1) Any history with child protection services?
2) Any agencies providing developmental services?

Possible causes:
1) Rule out abuse or neglect
2) Natural disease possibly related to existing conditions

Summary:

The initial inquiry produces the following details: mom and dad live with 2 children, ages 18 months, and a newborn. The decedent was last seen around 8:00 pm the following evening when fed by the mother. She had been well, no medical concerns recently, recent pediatric visit, did vomit over night in crib. She is not on any medications, but has prescription cold medicines in the home. Developmentally she is functioning around the age of 10 months. Parents report no abuse in the home. Father out of work. Decedent was premature (32 weeks). From the autopsy, gross findings show marked dehydration, and negative toxicology screen. No CPS history, but child receives numerous therapies from county agencies. Now examine the system. Father out of work (stressor #1), newborn in home (stressor #2), special needs child (stressor #3). Review of the last pediatric visit reveals that the child was doing fine at that time, but at autopsy had dropped 3½ pounds since the visit, resulting in the dehydration. Follow-up with mother reveals that she had been skipping some meals. Thus, a natural death with neglect as a contributing factor.

Case #2 —

17 year old male found dead in bed at home. No past medical history.

Inquiry:

1) Last Seen Alive?
2) Activities, circumstances in previous 24 hours?
3) Recent illness or complaints?
4) Any known drug history?
5) Medications?
6) Any recent events or changes?

Questions for pathologist:

1) Gross findings?
2) Toxicology?

Possible causes:

1) Rule out drug overdose?
2) Other natural disease?

Summary:

The initial inquiry reveals that the decedent was last seen after dinner watching TV, and went to bed around 10:30 pm. He was checked on by mother when he did not get up for school. No history of recent illness or complaints according to parents. He went to school the previous day, and basketball practice after school. Typical day with nothing out of the ordinary. He takes no medications and does not use drugs or alcohol. From the autopsy, a full tox screen reveals nothing, but the autopsy reveals myocarditis as the cause of death.

Case #3 —

15 year old male had seizure at school and later died. Illegal drugs found in his pocket.

Inquiry:

1) Medical history, specifically history related to seizures or recent illness?
2) Drug use history?
3) Activities in the 24 hours prior to death?

Questions for pathologists

1) Gross findings?
2) Toxicology?

Possible causes:

1) Overdose
2) Rule out seizure disorder
3) Other natural disease

Summary:

Unlike the previous two cases, the onset of symptoms in this case is witnessed. This may eliminate some questions, or may create more depending on the circumstances. In this case, the initial inquiry reveals little with no prior medical history or seizures, and no known drug use by the decedent. Reports indicate typical routines were followed the previous day and up until the seizure occurred. All hopes rest with the autopsy results: cause of death was concentric left ventricular hypertrophy, with a negative tox screen. The drugs can raise questions that should be addressed but in this case is an unrelated finding.

Case #4—

10 year old with a history of being sick within the past 36 hours prior to death. Found dead in bed at home.

Inquiry:

1) Recent symptoms and when they started?
2) Past medical history?

3) Last seen alive and activity at that time?
4) Activities in prior 24 hours?
5) Medications?
6) Reasons for not seeking treatment?

Questions for pathologist:
1) Gross findings?
2) Toxicology?

Possible causes:
1) Rule out toxin/poisoning
2) Rule out blunt force trauma
3) Other natural causes

Summary:

This history poses many questions, but initial inquires reveal little in the way of details. Mother reports that the decedent was vomiting and being lethargic, and she kept him hydrated thinking he may have the flu. No past medical history and had been playing normally up until 3 days prior. She did not think he was seriously ill and did not seek treatment. From the autopsy, negative tox screen, but acute appendicitis and peritonitis was listed as the cause of death. No history with outside agencies, however a report was made to CPS for possible neglect for not seeking treatment.

Chapter 5: Accidental Death Cases

Case #1 —

17 year old male found by father slumped over with a belt around his neck, attached to the doorknob of his bedroom door. Deceased was partially clothed, adult magazine located beside body, no history of depression or stress. Parents in the home at the time.

Inquiry:

1) Establish history of hanging activities, if known?
2) Activities that day?
3) Determine original position?
4) Reconstruct how decedent was found and what was done prior to arrival of first responders?

Questions for pathologist:

1) Gross findings?
2) Toxicology?

Possible causes:

1) Cause is known—hanging. Determination of manner will be the focus of the investigation, with it being either a suicide or accident.

Summary:

The initial inquiry reveals little from the family as far as history, but the friends do indicate some knowledge of him having attempted the hanging behavior before. Father went to his room after dinner and got no answer, then could not open the door. Body was moved by father pushing the door open. He took the belt off before calling 911. The autopsy shows findings consistent with hanging and a negative toxicology screen. Given no indicators for suicide, but indicators for experimental behavior, this case is ruled as an accidental death.

Case #2 —

14 year old with past history for use of Zoloft and alcohol. School history significant for known drug usage. Found dead in bed at home.

Inquiry:

1) Past medical history?
2) Recent medical issues or concerns?

3) Last seen alive?
4) Activities that day?
5) Medications at scene?
6) Drug history?

Questions for pathologist:

1) Gross findings?
2) Toxicology?

Questions for other agencies:

1) School history and involvement?
2) CPS history?
3) Mental health history, decedent and family?

Possible causes:

1) Rule out overdose
2) Other natural

Summary:

Unfortunately, the scene in this case yields little in the way of evidence as the decedent had no medications on him at the time, nor were there any present near the body. So the pertinent information comes through interviews with family present. Initially, the history provided is negative, no past medical history, regular routines, etc. Friends confirm they witnessed the decedent take something though they did not know what he took. Further questioning of the parents confirms prescriptions for Zoloft and admission that they knew he used it. All indicators point towards a toxicology case, which is confirmed by the final autopsy. However, the overdose was due to methadone. The parents have no prescriptions for methadone, so the focus turns towards the friends. Further questioning reveals one of them bought the pills from home to the party. Agency histories reveal involvement from both school and CPS. The source of the methadone was identified.

Case #3 —
9 week old female found deceased in bed with parents.

Inquiry:
1) Identify those in the bed?
2) Document each person's position in the bed?
3) Document height and weight of each person?
4) Photograph and document bedding, type of sleeping surface, and size of bed?
5) Document fluids on bedding and any fluids on clothing of co-sleepers?
6) Document position of decedent when placed in the bed and when found?
7) Note any indicators of alcohol or drug use?
8) Note signs of death, and if they confirm position of death?

Questions for pathologist:
1) Gross findings?
2) Any signs or pressure marks consistent with rollover?
3) Toxicology?

Possible causes:
1) SIDS
2) Other natural
3) Rule out overlay

Summary:
The initial inquiry produces three people in the bed, both parents and infant, with the infant between them on a double bed. The bedding was a light comforter and sheet. Both parents exceeded 200 lbs and were approximately 5'4" to 5'10". Infant was placed face up with head on the pillow, but found on its side below pillow, facing the mother's back. Small fluid stain on sheet and stain on upper shoulder of mom's nightshirt. No indicators of al-

cohol or drug usage in home or by report. Lividity appears consistent with the deceased being found on its side. Autopsy findings are negative, with negative toxicology. Given the physical evidence and scene details, this is ruled an asphyxial death by overlying.

Case #4—

5 year old male reportedly shot in home by sibling. Others present include children aged 4 and 8 years. Parents at store at time of shooting.

Inquiry:

1) Weapon description, ownership, and where was it found?
2) Circumstances leading to shooting?
3) Supervision?
4) How did the children get the gun?

Questions for pathologist:

1) Are wounds consistent with history?

Questions for agencies:

1) Prior CPS history?

Summary:

The initial inquiry immediately demonstrates no supervision. The sibling phoned 911 and the parents arrived home shortly before the ambulance arrived. Due to the scene being extremely chaotic, little was gathered at the time. Subsequent interviews with the children resulted in the following information: the two youngest were playing in the back bedroom (parents' room) and jumping on the bed. They were playing with their toy guns. They saw the gun on top of the dresser and climbed up to get it with the sibling pointing it at the decedent and pulling the trigger. The gun was a .38 pistol, registered to father and kept on top of the dresser. The autopsy findings are consistent with a close range gunshot wound to the head. There was no prior CPS history, although interviews with neighbors reported the children being left alone often.

Chapter 6: Suicidal Death Cases

Case #1 —

12 year old male found hanging in his bedroom from a bedpost with a rope.

Inquiry:

1) Scene reconstruction — position when found, hanging mechanism?
2) Circumstances — activities that day and leading up to finding the decedent?
3) Family history?
4) Social history?
5) Behavioral history?

Questions for pathologist:

1) Injuries consistent with history?
2) Toxicology?

Questions for agencies:

1) Mental health history?

Summary:

The initial inquiry yields important answers related to the death. The circumstances provided indicate the decedent was upset with the family regarding ongoing issues. The family history is significant for a plan to move causing an escalation in already existing behavior problems. The decedent's history is also positive for a prior suicide attempt. The scene reconstruction is consistent with autopsy findings. The tox screen was negative. Mental health records requested.

Case #2 —

14 year old female found in the garage by her mother with a gunshot wound to the head. Several notes recovered from the scene.

Inquiry:

1) Circumstances, activities, routines that day?
2) Family history?
3) Behavior history?
4) Social history?
5) Gun information?

Questions for pathologist:

1) Injuries consistent with scene?
2) Toxicology?

Summary:

The circumstances appear straight forward in this case. Mother reports that the decedent complained of being sick so she allowed her to stay at home. She was aware that she had a fight with her boyfriend the night before. She last saw her alive at 9:15 am before she left for church. Found her at approximately 12:30 when she came home. Decedent's history was negative for any indicators of depression or suicidal ideation, she was reportedly very popular and played sports. No significant history for drugs or alcohol use. The decedent left several notes, but gave no specific reasons for killing herself. The notes were full of apologies to friends and family. Gun was a .45 revolver that was not secured. Toxicology screen positive for alcohol, but negative for other substances. Autopsy findings consistent with self-inflicted gunshot wound.

Case #3 —

15 year old male verbalized that he would kill himself before he moved. Younger sibling found him in room hanging from a closet bar.

Inquiry:

1) Original position and/or reconstruction?
2) Behavior history?
3) Family history?
4) Social history?
5) Last seen alive?

Questions for pathologist:

1) Injury consistent with history?
2) Toxicology?

Summary:

Fortunately, we have a clear communication and can form the inquiry around that communication. The family history is confirmed for a plan to relocate. He had never previously made any threats to hurt or kill himself according to family, friends or school personnel. The timeframe from when his parents argued with him until his sibling found him was only approximately 15–20 minutes. He was cut down upon discovery. The autopsy findings were consistent with the history, with a negative tox screen.

Chapter 7: Homicide Cases

Case #1 —

EMS responded to call for an unresponsive 9 month old. Visible bruising, mother's boyfriend reported child fell from crib. Law enforcement notified and responded to the scene. Child pronounced at the hospital.

Inquiry:

1) Process scene?
2) Witness interviews?
3) Physical observations at hospital?

4) Identify red flags?
5) Obtain initial statement?
6) Last seen alive and by whom?
7) Who was with child at the time?
8) Timeline?

Questions for pathologist:

1) Findings consistent with history?
2) Internal injuries to correspond to external bruising?

Questions for agencies:

1) CPS history
2) Other agencies involved?

Summary:

We will start with the initial statement made by the boyfriend. He reports the child crying and he went upstairs to check on her and she had fallen out of the crib and was lying on the floor. Neighbors reported hearing the infant crying. Ten to fifteen minutes later he heard the ambulance arrive. Mom is interviewed at the hospital and reports she left the residence around 11:30 after giving the child a bottle and putting her in her crib. Where was she going? To work. Who was left to care for the child? New boyfriend, who had moved in one month prior. Red flags at this point are male caregiver, and history of a fall. The scene itself was unkempt, but no visible signs of injuries or blood around the crib and bedroom. At the hospital, the child is examined and photographed. Visible injuries include a large bruise near the neck, bruising to the abdominal area and forehead. The bruises appear to be old and new. No other visible trauma. The boyfriend admits to dropping the child while playing, and goes into great detail about previous times he had accidentally dropped her. Two things wrong with this 'confession': 1) It doesn't explain the injuries observed or the fact the child is dead, 2) He is providing information about things he was *not* asked about. He later admits to shaking and slamming her. He is charged that night with first degree murder and felony child abuse. Autopsy findings include multiple skull fractures and mesenteric hemorrhage. Cause of death is ruled Blunt Force Trauma of the head and abdomen. Here is the problem. He mentioned slamming her once. And he never gave any explanations for abdominal injuries. Lesson: Wait at least for preliminary autopsy results in possible abuse cases to know exactly what you are dealing with. Mom admitted she had noticed bruising on the child but the boyfriend always explained them.

Case #2 —

16 year old female presented to ER with abdominal pains and bleeding. Examination showed recent birth. Authorities were notified and contacted family. A search was conducted at the home and a deceased newborn was discovered in the trash.

Inquiry:

1) Family history—was pregnancy known?
2) Pregnancy history—prenatal care, concealment, father, when conceived?
3) Birth details?
4) Timeline for that day, how long between delivery and ER?

Questions for pathologist:

1) Was infant born alive?
2) Cause of death?
3) Gestational age?

Possible causes:

1) Rule out fetal death
2) Rule out potential natural disease or prematurity

Summary:

The family history revealed that no one in the home knew that the girl was pregnant. They did know she had a boyfriend. The girl reported that she thought she might be pregnant. She estimates that she was close to eight or nine months along. She saw no doctor at any point. She concealed the pregnancy from everyone except the boyfriend. She reported that she was having abdominal pains and thought she had to go to the bathroom. She delivered the baby in the tub and did not cut the cord. She reported that the baby gasped, but she was not sure it was alive. She panicked, and wrapped the baby in a plastic bag. She cleaned up and put it in the trash. Autopsy findings confirmed a live birth of an approximately 37 week old infant with no anatomic findings. The cause of death was ruled asphyxiation, given the history of being put in the plastic bag.

Case #3 —

2 year old presented to ER. History of vomiting, no external trauma, some bruising noted on forehead and child was wet.

Inquiry:
1) Last seen alive and by whom?
2) Past medical history?
3) Circumstances?
4) Clarify 'wet'?
5) Reconstruction?

Questions for pathologist:
1) Findings?
2) Are they consistent with history and/or reconstruction?
3) Cause of death?

Questions for agencies:
1) CPS history?
2) Other records?

Possible causes:
1) Drowning
2) Abuse
3) Asphyxiation

Summary:

Lots of idiosyncrasies here to weed through. Circumstances reported by the caregiver are as follows: He had arrived home just after lunch. The two year old said she felt sick so he told her to go to the bathroom. The oldest was already in her room watching TV. He says he hears her get sick and then he goes in to check on her. He puts her in the tub to clean her off and she goes limp in his arms. He pumps on her stomach thinking she might be choking. He then grabs her and puts her in the car and heads to the hospital. No past medical history for the decedent. Autopsy findings include, blunt force trauma to head and abdomen and aspiration of gastric contents. The cause is listed as asphyxiation due to drowning. So how did we get here? The mesenteric hemorrhage was not sufficient to have caused her death. The bruising and blunt force trauma was both old and new and was not sufficient to have caused her death, nor was the aspiration. So what pulls this information all together? A forensic interview of the oldest child revealed she witnessed him drown her sister in the tub.

Chapter 8: Undetermined Cases

Case #1 —

4 month old found dead in bed with mother and sibling.

Inquiry:

1) Last seen alive and by whom?
2) Positions in bed?
3) Sizes of those in bed?
4) Position of infant when placed and found?
5) Size of bed?
6) Past medical history?
7) Sleep patterns?

Questions for pathologist:
1) Findings?
2) Toxicology?

Possible causes:
1) Overlay
2) SIDS
3) Other

Summary:

The initial inquiry reveals an average sized parent (5'4", 135 lbs) and 40 lb sibling on a twin bed with the decedent. Infant was last seen alive around 4:30 pm when it last ate (bottle fed). Infant was placed face up, with mother between the two children, sibling was on the wall side and baby on the other. Infant found in same position. No past medical history, mother reported being a light sleeper and heard no sounds from the infant after it ate and fell asleep. The autopsy and toxicology results were negative. As overlay could not be definitively ruled out, this case was ruled undetermined.

Case #2 —

13 month old found deceased in crib.

Inquiry:
1) Circumstances?
2) Who is in the house?
3) Last seen alive and by whom?
4) Past medical history?
5) Crib exam?
6) Positions?
7) Temperature in house?

Questions for pathologist:

1) Findings?
2) Toxicology?
3) Cause of death?

Questions for other agencies:

1) CPS history
2) Other agencies

Summary:

Members of the household include two other children ages 4–10, and mom and dad. The oldest child reported mom going in to get the baby and coming out screaming the baby wasn't breathing. Law Enforcement did respond to the scene and processed it. No past medical history. Crib appeared in good working condition, dirty linens but no extraneous bedding. Just sheets and blanket and onesie on the child. The ambient temperature in the house and room was 72 degrees. The child was last seen alive around 2:00 am. Baby was put down face up and found on its side. No true investigation was conducted beyond the initial scene. Autopsy findings and tox were negative. No anatomic cause of death. LE did inquire about a CPS history which was very lengthy. Case was ruled as undetermined due to the inability to determine either cause or manner of death.

Case #3 —

18 month old reportedly lethargic at home.

Inquiry:

1) Timeline for symptoms?
2) Activities that day?
3) Signs of trauma or illness?
4) Past medical history?
5) Any evidence at scene to suggest circumstances?
6) History from both caretaker?

Questions for pathologist:
1) Findings?
2) Any signs of abuse?
3) Toxicology?

Questions for agencies:
1) CPS history
2) LE history

Summary:

In this case the inquiry and agency check come together quickly to provide direction to the investigation. The timeline begins at the child's residence earlier in the morning. By mother's report, the child was fine. She put the child on the couch so she could take a shower and go to work. After the shower, she notices the child 'not acting right' and only wanting to lie on the couch. She got concerned after about an hour and called 911. There was no past or recent history of illness or symptoms other than lethargy and not eating. The scene was dirty and prescription medications were seized from the home. There were no signs of trauma or neglect with the decedent. The autopsy findings were negative, however as all investigative information pointed to a possible toxicology case, standard and additional analyses were run. The results came back positive for a toxic amount of methadone. Mother did have a prescription, and admitted that she could have left them out. It could not be determined how the child ingested the medication, so the manner was ruled undetermined.

HIPAA

These guidelines were written specifically for law enforcement in the state of North Carolina. The interaction of laws may differ across states. It is recommended that law enforcement consult with their legal representatives if there are questions about the application of HIPAA.

Purpose

The development and implementation of the Health Insurance Portability and Accountability Act (HIPAA) has been occurring over the last several years, but only recently went into effect as of April 14, 2003. The long-term ramifications of this federal legislation are unclear; however, immediate effects are already being felt by local and state law enforcement agencies.

Health care entities are being educated on the regulations, with emphasis on the civil and criminal penalties attached to wrongful disclosures. While both federal and state regulations are clear with regards to investigative efforts, reluctance to disclose ANY Protected Health Information (PHI) is the result. Our purpose in developing guidelines for law enforcement is to 1) present the HIPAA regulations that directly and indirectly apply to law enforcement efforts in a death investigation, 2) discuss the implications for death investigations and obtaining information, and 3) provide recommendations for applying both state and HIPAA mandates appropriately to death investigations.

Introduction

The Health Insurance Portability and Accountability Act (1996, PL 104-191) was created to ensure health coverage when employees change jobs (portability), protect the integrity, confidentiality, and availability of health data (accountability), and set national standards for how health information is transmitted and protected. While the road was paved with good intentions, gravel and potholes mar the actual interpretation of this federal act.

The end result is federal legislation that must co-exist with existing state laws. Thus, there are preemptions of state law by the federal regulations, exemptions by state law to the preemptions of the federal regulations, and state law provisions which have to be examined individually against federal regulations to determine which applies. So how do we know which is correct? That is not yet clear. Interpretations vary across covered entities, attorneys, and agencies needing specific protected information. Unfortunately, the courts will most likely be the determining force as the source for orders and warrants to obtain information, as well as to interpret the intent and application of the laws. Ideally, the initial fervor and reluctance to share ANY information will die down, allowing entities to better understand and apply the mandates. In the meantime, we will look at the specifics of HIPAA and how it can be applied in death investigations.

Definitions

PHI (Protected Health Information) — All Individually Identifiable Health Information and other information on treatment and care that is transmitted or maintained in any form or medium
Use — The sharing, employment, application, utilization, examination, or analysis of such information within an entity that maintains such information
Disclosure — Release or divulgence of information by an entity to persons or organizations outside of that entity

Authorization—The mechanism for obtaining consent from a patient for the use and disclosure of health information for a purpose that is not treatment, payment, or health care operations or not for other permitted disclosures such as those required by law and for public health purposes

Minimum Necessary—When using PHI, a covered entity must make all reasonable efforts to limit itself to "the minimum necessary to accomplish the intended purpose of the use, disclosure, or request"

Health Plan—An individual or group plan that provides, or pays the cost of, medical care

Health Care Provider—Any person or organization that furnishes, bills, or is paid for health care services or supplies (such as DSS, EMS, Mental Health, Health Departments, etc)

Health Care Clearinghouse—A public or private entity that processes or facilitates the processing of nonstandard data elements of health information into standard data elements

Covered Entities—Those entities that must comply with HIPAA regulations: Health Plans, Health Care Providers, and Health Care Clearinghouses

Statutes

** NOTE: Only the applicable portions of the statutes are presented.

160.203 General rule and exceptions

A standard, requirement, or implementation specification adopted under this subchapter that is contrary to a provision of State law preempts the provision of State law. This general rule applies, except if one or more of the following conditions is met:

(c) The provision of State law, including State procedures established under such law, as applicable, provides for the reporting of disease or injury, child abuse, birth, or death, or for the conduct of public health surveillance, investigation, or intervention.

164.502 Uses and disclosures of protected health information: general rules

(a) Standard—A covered entity may not use or disclose protected health information, except as permitted or required by this subpart or by subpart C of part 160 of this subchapter.

    1) Permitted uses and disclosures—A covered entity is permitted to use or disclose protected health information as follows:

        i.   As permitted by and in compliance with this section, 164.512 or 164.514 (e), (f), or (g).

    2) Required disclosures—A covered entity is required to disclose protected health information:

        i.   To an individual, when requested under, and as required by 164.524 or 164.528; and

        ii. When required by the Secretary under subpart C of part 160 of this subchapter to investigate or determine the covered entity's compliance with this subpart.

(b) Standard: minimum necessary

    1) Minimum necessary applies

    2) Minimum necessary does not apply—This requirement does not apply to:

        (v.) Uses or disclosures that are required by law, as described by 164.512 (a)

164.512 Uses and disclosures for which an authorization or opportunity to agree or object is not required.

A covered entity may use or disclose protected health information without the written authorization of the individual, as described in 164.508, or the opportunity for the individual to agree or object as described in 164.510, in the situations covered by this section, subject to the applicable requirements of this section. When the covered entity is required by this section to inform the individual of, or when the individual may agree to, a use of disclosure permitted by this section, the covered entity's information and the individual's agreement may be given orally.

(a) Standard: uses and disclosures required by law

1) A covered entity may use or disclose protected health information to the extent that such use or disclosure is required by law and the use or disclosure complies with and is limited to the relevant requirements of such law.

2) A covered entity must meet the requirements described in paragraph (c), (e), or (f) of this section for uses or disclosures required by law.

(b) Standard: uses and disclosures for public health activities

1) Permitted disclosures: A covered entity may disclose protected health information for the public health activities and purposes described in this paragraph to:

i. A public health authority that is authorized by law to collect or receive such information for the purpose of preventing or controlling disease, injury, or disability, including, but not limited to, the reporting of disease, injury, vital events such as birth or death, and the conduct of public health surveillance, public health investigations, and public health interventions; or, at the direction of a public health authority, to an official of a foreign government agency that is acting in collaboration with a public health authority;

ii. A public health authority or other appropriate government authority authorized by law to receive reports of child abuse or neglect

2) Permitted uses: If the covered entity also is a public health authority, the covered entity is permitted to use protected health information in all cases in which it is permitted to disclose such information for public health activities under paragraph (b)(1) of this section.

(c) Standard: disclosures about victims of abuse, neglect or domestic violence

1) Permitted disclosures: Except for reports of child abuse or neglect permitted by (b)(1)(ii) of this section, a covered entity may disclose protected health information about an individual whom the covered entity reasonably believes to be a victim of abuse, neglect, or domestic violence to a government authority, including a social service or protective services agency, authorized by law to receive reports of such abuse, neglect, or domestic violence:

   i.   To the extent the disclosure is required by law and the disclosure complies with and is limited to the relevant requirements of such law;

   ii. If the individual agrees to the disclosure; or

   iii. To the extent the disclosure is expressly authorized by statute or regulation and:

      A. The covered entity, in the exercise of professional judgment, believes the disclosure is necessary to prevent serious harm to the individual or other potential victims; or

      B. If the individual is unable to agree because of incapacity, a law enforcement or other public official authorized to receive the report represents that the protected health information for which disclosure is sought is not intended to be used against the individual and that an immediate enforcement activity that depends upon the disclosure would be materially and adversely affected by waiting until the individual is able to agree to the disclosure.

2) Informing the individual: A covered entity that makes a disclosure permitted by paragraph (c)(1) of this section

must promptly inform the individual that such a report has been or will be made, except if:

    i. The covered entity, in the exercise of professional judgment, believes informing the individual would place the individual at risk of serious harm; or

    ii. The covered entity would be informing a personal representative, and the covered entity reasonably believes the personal representative is responsible for the abuse, neglect, or other injury, and that informing such person would not be in the best interests of the individual as determined by the covered entity, in the exercise of professional judgment.

(d) Standard: uses and disclosures for health oversight activities

(e) Standard: disclosures for judicial and administrative proceedings

    1) Permitted disclosures: A covered entity may disclose protected health information in the course of any judicial or administrative proceeding

    2) Other uses and disclosures under this section: The provisions of this paragraph do not supersede other provisions of this section that otherwise permit or restrict uses or disclosures of protected health information.

(f) Standard: disclosures for law enforcement purposes

    1) Permitted disclosures: pursuant to process and as otherwise required by law. A covered entity may disclose protected health information:

        i. As required by law including laws that require the reporting of certain types of wounds or other physical injuries, except for laws subject to paragraph (b)(1)(ii) or (c)(1)(i) of this section; or

        ii. In compliance with and as limited by the relevant requirements of:

A. A court order or court-ordered warrant, or a subpoena or summons issued by a judicial officer;

B. A grand jury subpoena; or

C. An administrative request, including an administrative subpoena or summons, a civil or an authorized investigative demand, or similar process authorized under law, provided that:

    1. The information sought is relevant and material to a legitimate law enforcement inquiry;

    2. The request is specific and limited in scope to the extent reasonably practicable in light of the purpose for which the information is sought; and

    3. De-identified information could not reasonably be used.

2) Permitted disclosures: limited information for identification and location purposes. Except for disclosures required by law as permitted by paragraph (f)(1) of this section, a covered entity may disclose protected health information in response to a law enforcement official's request for such information for the purpose of identifying or locating a suspect, fugitive, material witness, or missing person, provided that:

i. The covered entity may disclose only the following information:

    A. Name and address;

    B. Date and place of birth;

    C. Social security number;

    D. ABO blood type and rh factor;

    E. Type of injury;

    F. Date and time of treatment;

G. Date and time of death, if applicable; and

H. A description of distinguishing physical characteristics, including height, weight, gender, race, hair and eye color, presence or absence of facial hair, scars, and tattoos.

ii. Except as permitted by paragraph (f)(2)(i) of this section, the covered entity may not disclose for the purposes of identification or location under paragraph (f)(2) of this section any protected health information related to the individual's DNA or DNA analysis, dental records, or typing, samples or analysis of body fluids or tissues.

3) Permitted disclosure: victims of a crime. Except for disclosures required by law as permitted by paragraph (f)(1) of this section, a covered entity may disclose protected health information in response to a law enforcement official's request for such information about an individual who is or is suspected to be a victim of a crime, other than disclosures that are subject to paragraph (b) or (c) of this section, if:

i. The individual agrees to the disclosure; or

ii. The covered entity is unable to obtain the individual's agreement because of incapacity or other emergency circumstance, provided that:

A. The law enforcement official represents that such information is needed to determine whether a violation of law by a person other than the victim has occurred, and such information is not intended to be used against the victim;

B. The law enforcement official represents that immediate law enforcement activity that depends upon the disclosure would be materially and adversely affected by waiting until the individual is able to agree to the disclosure; and

C. The disclosure is in the best interests of the individual as determined by the covered entity, in the exercise of professional judgment.

4) Permitted disclosure: decedents. A covered entity may disclose protected health information about an individual who has died to a law enforcement official for the purpose of alerting law enforcement of the death of the individual if the covered entity has a suspicion that such death may have resulted from criminal conduct.

5) Permitted disclosure: crime on premises. A covered entity may disclose to a law enforcement official protected health information that the covered entity believes in good faith constitutes evidence of criminal conduct that occurred on the premises of the covered entity.

6) Permitted disclosure: reporting crime in emergencies.

i. A covered health care provider providing emergency health care in response to a medical emergency, other than such emergency on the premises of the covered health care provider, may disclose protected health information to a law enforcement official if such disclosure appears necessary to alert law enforcement to:

A. The commission and nature of a crime;

B. The location of such crime or of the victim(s) of such crime; and

C. The identity, description, and location of the perpetrator of such crime.

ii. If a covered health care provider believes that the medical emergency described in paragraph (f)(6)(i) of this section is the result of abuse, neglect, or domestic violence of the individual in need of emergency health care, paragraph (f)(6)(i) of this section does not apply and any disclosure to a law enforcement official for law enforcement purposes is subject to paragraph (c) of this section.

(g) Standard: uses and disclosures about decedents

  1) Coroners and medical examiners: A covered entity may disclose protected health information to a coroner or medical examiner for the purpose of identifying a deceased person, determining a cause of death, or other duties as authorized by law. A covered entity that also performs the duties of a coroner or medical examiner may use protected health information for the purposes described in this paragraph.

  2) Funeral directors

(h) Standard: uses and disclosures for cadaveric organ, eye or tissue donation purposes

(i) Standard: uses and disclosures for research purposes

(j) Standard: uses and disclosures to avert a serious threat to health or safety

  1) Permitted disclosures: A covered entity may, consistent with applicable law and standards of ethical conduct, use or disclose protected health information, if the covered entity, in good faith, believes the use or disclosure:

    i. A. Is necessary to prevent or lessen a serious and imminent threat to the health or safety of a person or the public; and

       B. Is to a person or persons reasonably able to prevent or lessen the threat, including the target of the threat; or

    ii. Is necessary for law enforcement authorities to identify or apprehend an individual:

       A. Because of a statement by an individual admitting participation in a violent crime that the covered entity reasonably believes may have caused serious physical harm to the victim; or

B. Where it appears from all the circumstances that the individual has escaped from a correctional institution or from lawful custody (164.501)

2) Use or disclosure not permitted: A use or disclosure pursuant to paragraph (j)(1)(ii)(A) of this section may not be made if the information described in paragraph (j)(1)(ii)(A) of this section is learned by the covered entity:

i. In the course of treatment to affect the propensity to commit the criminal conduct that is the basis for the disclosure under paragraph (j)(1)(ii)(A) of this section, or counseling or therapy; or

ii. Through a request by the individual to initiate or to be referred for the treatment, counseling, or therapy described in paragraph (j)(2)(i) of this section.

3) Limit on information that may be disclosed: A disclosure made pursuant to paragraph (j)(1)(ii)(A) of this section shall contain only the statement described in paragraph (j)(1)(ii)(A) of this section and the protected health information described in paragraph (f)(2)(i) of this section.

4) Presumption of good faith belief: A covered entity that uses or discloses protected health information pursuant to paragraph (j)(1) of this section is presumed to have acted in good faith with regard to a belief described in paragraph (j)(1)(i) or (ii) of this section, if the belief is based upon the covered entity's actual knowledge or in reliance on a credible representation by a person with apparent knowledge or authority.

(k) Standard: uses and disclosures for specialized government functions

(l) Standard: disclosures for workers' compensation

Implications

160.203 General rule and exceptions

The general rule and exceptions section makes it clear that HIPAA is the overriding mandate to follow. Provision (c) describes the State Law exemptions to the general rule. As this applies directly to the reporting of fatalities, this should not affect law enforcement. While there are existing problems with regards to notification in the event of a death, these are largely local communication gaps and are not related to HIPAA. As a public heath authority, the medical examiner system is exempt under the HIPAA regulations. Thus, local medical examiners should be able to continue to conduct inquiries and investigations as they typically would, which should include contacting law enforcement.

Unfortunately, it appears that many are not reading beyond this statute. There is an overwhelming reaction of 'when in doubt, do not give it out'. It is critical for law enforcement to know what the regulations are and when to question a refusal to disclose information as part of an active death investigation.

164.502 Uses and disclosures of protected health information: general rules

This section defines permitted versus required disclosures. The implication behind these standards being that while an entity *may* disclose PHI under this subchapter, they may not necessarily *have* to disclose anything. This is particularly relevant given that 164.512, which includes the standards for law enforcement purposes and decedents, is specifically listed under permitted disclosures.

The minimum necessary standard simply means that the covered entity must make every reasonable effort to provide the requesting agency with the bare minimum. The standard does not apply to disclosures required by law. However, the standard specifically cites 164.512 (a). So how the minimum necessary applies to sections b–l of that section is open to interpretation.

164.512 Uses and disclosures for which an authorization or opportunity to agree or object is not required

(a) Standard: uses and disclosures required by law — The item that stands out with this standard is, that the disclosure must be *limited* to the relevant requirements of the law. So it appears that entities may disclose information to the letter of the law, meaning the requests need to be for exactly what is needed. If it is not written in there, you can bet it will not be provided.

(b) Standard: uses and disclosures for public health activities — This section allows for the exchange of information between health care providers and medical examiners. There is little room for misinterpretation here, though a few calls have been made regarding nursing staff refusals to disclose. Medical examiners can issue administrative subpoenas if necessary.

(c) Standard: disclosures about victims of abuse, neglect, or domestic violence — The State Law requiring reporting of suspicions of abuse or neglect trumps HIPAA. The provisions clearly stipulate disclosures when the threat of harm to the victim exists, or if an investigation will be compromised without the information. In addition, entities do not have to disclose to a representative for the victim (e.g., the abusive parent) if they are the suspected perpetrator. While things tend to move rapidly at the time, mutual agreement on this section should expedite the sharing of information.

(d) Standard: uses and disclosures for health oversight activities

(e) Standard: disclosures for judicial and administrative proceedings — If a death investigation has proceeded to this stage, there should be no arguments for obtaining records.

(f) Standard: disclosures for law enforcement purposes — Section (1) under this subchapter covers the statute for physicians to report certain types of wounds and injuries (G.S. 90-21.20), as well as requests required by law. Section (2) delves into information sought for identification and location purposes. As problems obtaining this type of information are already occurring, it is important that law enforcement know this section thoroughly. It is specific with regards to what the information is for and what can be disclosed. While identifying characteristics are invaluable in identifying some bodies, decomposed cases or skeletal remains may require DNA or dental records. The statute clearly states information related to DNA, dental records, or fluids and tissues cannot be disclosed. Section (3) deals with a victim or suspected victim of a crime. As we deal exclusively with the dead, an agreement by the victim to disclose is obviously not an option. Therefore, law enforcement will have to show that the information is needed to rule out criminal activity in the death, or that the investigation will be compromised without the information. This leads directly to Section (4) regarding decedents. You will notice the statute specifically states that law enforcement can be alerted about a death 'if the covered entity has a suspicion that such death may have resulted from criminal conduct'. Two potential problems exist here. First, that is the opinion of the covered entity, which is not likely to have all the information necessary to make that judgment, nor is that necessarily their role. Second, it implies that seemingly accidental, suicidal, or natural deaths are *not* a law enforcement concern. Therefore, as law enforcement is charged with investigating all deaths as potentially suspicious until proven otherwise, Section (3) should hopefully assist in obtaining the necessary information. Section (6) relates to situations involving EMS. We are already being informed that law enforcement is being refused information at scenes by EMS personnel, requiring court orders to get ambulance call sheets and reports. The statute houses disclosures under 'crime', similar to Section (4). With respect to a fatality on scene, or a person transported that later dies, it is unclear whether EMS personnel *have* to provide any information to law enforcement without clear evidence of criminal conduct, with the exception of abuse, neglect or domestic violence.

(g) Standard: uses and disclosures about decedents—This section
    reiterates G.S. 130A-385 Duties of the medical examiner

Recommendations

We really have no way of knowing how this intermingling of
federal and state legislation will play out until it is taken to the
courts for interpretation. In the meantime, we must deal with it
on a case-by-case basis the best we can. Following are several recommendations that law enforcement agencies can use and/or adapt
for assimilating HIPAA into everyday law enforcement activities
and active death investigations.

1) Meeting of the minds—Department attorneys should meet
   with legal and staff representatives from the covered entities, particularly hospitals and county EMS, to discuss the
   statutes and policies for exchanging information to the
   benefit of all. The end result should be a written document all parties agree on.
2) Specificity—Any court orders, warrants, subpoenas, or
   other judicial or official requests for information should
   be as specific as possible. 'Fishing expeditions' without
   solid justification are not likely to be accepted by covered
   entities. Your reasons for needing the information will
   need to be just as clear as how it will be used.
3) Documentation—If departments have an existing request
   form, modify it to include the specific HIPAA regulations
   related to the information needed. For example, the OCME
   request for medical records includes the following statement; "We request the following records as part of our investigation under the authority granted by NC G.S.
   130A-385." If modifying an already existing document is not
   possible, consider having a letter drafted or template created that states your agencies purpose, the nature of the
   investigation, the HIPAA regulation that allows the entity
   to disclose the requested information, and agency contact

information. The Centers for Disease Control has sample
letters available on their website (see Resources).

4) Availability—Law enforcement personnel should keep a
copy of the applicable HIPAA regulations where they can
be easily accessed in the event questions arise during an
investigation. A conversation and professional explanation
between two parties could potentially avoid an unnecessary court order for information.

Resources

www.hipaa.org
www.medicalprivacy.unc.edu—Excellent legal interpretations of
the regulations and potential impact.
http://www.dirm.state.nc.us/hipaa
http://www.cdc.gov/mmwr—Do a search for HIPAA on the site
and it will list several appendices available. This will include
the sample letters mentioned above. They were available as of
May 2, 2003.

GLOSSARY

Abandonment — This term refers to a mother leaving a newborn after birth. She may leave it unattended or murder and dispose of it.

Child — Defined in this text as decedents aged 17 years and younger.

Cause — The physical findings that led to the death.

Contusion — Bruise to tissue, externally or internally.

Coroner — Typically an elected official, coroners may or may not be physicians. They perform similar functions as medical examiners providing support and expertise to medicolegal investigations, to include autopsies in certain systems. Some states operate under a coroner system or combination medical examiner/coroner system.

Forensic pathologist — A forensic pathologist is a physician who has specialized in forensic pathology and passed certification boards in that particular specialty. They can serve as medical examiners as well.

Homicide — One person taking the life of another person, by action or intention.

Manner — The circumstances by which a death occurred.

Mechanism — A process or object responsible for or related to a death.

Medical examiner — Medical examiners are typically physicians appointed to perform investigations into the circumstances of a death. Some states have a state administered medical examiner system and others have a county administered system. Depending on the system, medical examiners can perform autopsies or contract with pathologists to perform the autopsies. Medical examiners may or may not be a forensic pathologist.

Prone—Face down position.

Supine—On the back.

Surrender—Refers to the safe and secure surrender of a newborn to proper authorities under existing mandates.

Viability—Age at which a fetus can exist outside of the womb with no mechanical support.

Index